Blacktrekking:

My Journey Living in Latin America

Stephanie Claytor

www.blacktrekking.com

Facebook.com/blacktrekking

Twitter.com/blacktrekking

Instagram.com/blacktrekking

Blacktrekking@gmail.com

Edited, Formatted, and Published via *iWrite4orU*: www.iWrite4orU.com

Cover Designed and Formatted by: Alex Claytor Davis

Print ISBN: 978-0-9998842-3-2

Library of Congress Control Number: 2019908074

Author based in Lakeland, Florida

Printed in the United States of America

Stephanie Claytor

Stephanie Claytor

Introduction

From dancing to bachata music under the stars to parrandas and carnival, this book has tips for living abroad in Latin America. It's an entirely different experience than visiting somewhere for a week. While I share with you some of the enjoyable memories I have of exploring the Dominican Republic and Colombia, I'll also provide tips for staying safe as you embark on this life-changing adventure.

There's a ton of wonderful things I could say about my experience living in Colombia and the Dominican Republic. The music, the food, and the dancing were some of the things I enjoyed the most. I also wanted to share with you the part of the story that's often left out of most travel books, and from a perspective that rarely has a seat at the table.

After blogging for ten months about my experience living in Colombia, I decided to transform my blog into a book. I wanted to share my journey of living abroad, particularly from the point of view of a woman of color. In this book, you'll read things that I witnessed, from my experiences dating, living with a host family, and teaching English, and I'll share how it made me feel. Also, I left some key words and phrases in this book in Spanish, because they're key words and phrases you need to know when visiting these countries. This book is about the reality of living abroad—the good, the bad, and the ugly. Also, you'll read about destinations I'd recommend visiting, especially if you're as interested in learning about the African diaspora as I am.

This journey for me began when I was in the eighth grade, learning Spanish. I made it a goal of mine to become fluent after visiting California when I was 10 years old, and I found it difficult to communicate with many of the strangers my family encountered when we asked for directions. I had grown up in suburban Cleveland, Ohio, where back then everything was black or white. Visiting California made me realize there was an entirely different world out there, and I didn't want to be left out.

It wasn't until college that I realized taking Spanish classes and listening to reggaeton music wasn't sufficient. For me, I had to be immersed in the culture and forced to use the language on a daily basis. That's the reason I decided to move abroad, not once but twice. From performing in a Latin dance troupe in college to having many friends that spoke the language, Spanish slowly came natural to me. I knew when I was dreaming in Spanish that I had accomplished my goal.

And now, I'll share with you this wonderful journey; it's a journey full of ups and downs, setbacks and heartbreaks, but most importantly, a journey that I learned from and a journey that made me the woman I am today.

Chapter 1:
This Is A Different World

A month before I was to leave for Colombia in 2010, a dean was murdered on the campus where I was supposed to teach. Also, that same university claimed it couldn't pay my wages. So, the agency I contracted with told me I wouldn't be going to Cali, and instead I would be placed in Bogotá. I was so upset because I had my heart set on living in the city with good weather and a vibrant Afro-Colombian community, but I dealt with it. That was my first lesson in setting high expectations and then having them ruined. Living in Colombia, there was a lot that was beyond my control.

On the plane ride over there, the coldness gripped me. It felt like I was the only black person on the plane; no one greeted me or talked to me. Here I was traveling alone to this foreign country where I didn't know anyone and the plane ride didn't make it any easier. I was terrified about what I was getting myself into. And the flight was long! Five hours from Newark—the longest flight I'd ever been on.

When I arrived in Colombia, I was picked up at the airport by the program's staff. It was a Sunday night and dark and dreary outside. The streets were vacant. No one was walking outside. There wasn't any music playing, and worst of all, there weren't any palm trees. Instead, there were several buildings with graffiti all over them. They weren't bright colored like in the islands. I knew right away this was no Dominican Republic; it was a whole different ball game.

Despite the dark gloomy streets, I felt a lot safer than I thought I would during my first night in Bogotá. After all, my mother thought I was headed into a war zone and wasn't happy about me moving there. During my first phone call home, she told me to watch out for the cocaine. In her mind, it was everywhere and lots of people were using it. She got this idea from watching the American news outlets and movies. I assured her it wasn't that bad and what she suggested was wrong. During my entire time there, I believe I saw one person sniffing it on the street corner when the clubs let out. Other than that, I didn't see anyone using it in plain sight.

To me, Bogotá felt like living in any other big city, such as New York or Washington DC. During the day, there were people everywhere. Hundreds. The sidewalks were always packed with people walking to work, selling stuff on the sidewalks, and the homeless begging for money. Every day, thousands of people packed their bus rapid transit system called the TransMilenio. It was especially packed during rush hour. The streets were always jam-packed with cars and people honking their horns, cutting each other off. I didn't dare bother to ever try to drive anywhere. During my first week, I didn't feel like anyone was trying to attack me or take my things like I had been warned. There were police officers everywhere, and there were random checkpoints. The U.S. embassy staff conducted a meeting with the group I was there with to provide survival tips. We couldn't be naïve.

One of the main concerns was taxis. We were advised to avoid taking taxis alone, especially at night. We learned that if we boarded the wrong taxi, foreigner or Colombian, we could be taken on what they called a "paseo millonario". Basically, if we got into the wrong taxi, criminals could take us down random streets at a high rate of speed and into a dark, vacant lot or alley. Another criminal could enter the taxi, bop us upside the head, and take all of our stuff. Then they could drug us. Supposedly scopolamine was the criminal's drug of choice. The embassy staff warned us it was a drug that rendered a person incapable of free will and it could be transferred by touching or be added to foods and drinks. The security advisers went on to say that the criminals could administer the drug and then take us to ATMs and force us to liquidate our accounts. The "paseo millonario was basically an express kidnapping.

It wasn't the first time I had heard about this crime. I had talked to a girl who was in my program a few years prior who survived it. She was Colombian-American. She made the mistake of taking her laptop and iPhone with her to La Zona Rosa, an area full of ritzy nightclubs in Bogotá. She met with a group of friends and then wanted to go home around 8PM, shortly after nightfall. She went to the official taxi line and was waiting for a ride, but her friend's Colombian boyfriend told her she didn't need to wait, and waved down a cab on the street that wasn't an official one affiliated with a company. She said she got into the car with her expensive electronics in plain view. Then, after the driver took off, she said she noticed he was not driving in the direction of her home. Bogotá is a huge city, about a two-hour drive from the northern end to the southern end. Many professionals have never even visited the southern part of city.

When she told him, "Hey, this isn't the way home", she recalled him picking up speed. Next thing she knew, they stopped in a vacant lot and someone got in the back and hit her upside her head. She said they took her laptop, which had all of her research papers, her money, her phone, everything. Then, they left her in this lot. She had no idea where she was. But she lived to tell about it.

So, the lesson learned from my first days there was to never take a taxi alone at night, and always call for a taxi or go to the taxi stand. Never hop in a taxi off of the streets. Also, there were stories of people bringing knives on buses and robbing people. We were advised to stay in the cities and ride the TransMilenio and not to frequent the countryside. And never take a bus across the country because they couldn't confirm what could happen.

Of course, while I was there, I never was kidnapped or witnessed any robberies on the bus. It was something I knew could happen, but I never had any problems. I also listened to the State Department's guidance. Remember, I was there in 2010, when Colombia had just become safer for people to visit. Hopefully, it has gotten better since then.

Back then, pickpocketers were rampant. Our bags and purses had to have zippers and I learned to hold the zipper when I was on the TransMilenio. I always wore my backpack in front of my body. Every time I walked out of the confines of my apartment, I was on alert. We had to be. I'll never forget the day I was walking near the downtown area of Bogotá and I saw this teen boy carrying a big, bloody butcher knife. Two police officers had grabbed him by his shoulders and were dragging him down the street. The journalist in me wanted to know what happened, but the foreigner in me told me to keep walking, don't ask questions, and get out of the way.

There was also a phrase the Colombians lived by, "No dar papaya." It literally means "don't give the papaya", but for Colombians, it means not to put yourself in a position where someone can take advantage of you. It's a warning to be careful or to avoid setting yourself up or making yourself a target, which to them is "dando papaya". They interpret the phrase as "don't give someone access to your valuables if you don't want them taken away", because they'll take them and it'll be your fault because you gave them the opportunity. Basically, be proactive in preventing theft. Don't leave your doors open, or walk around with money or a cell phone hanging out of your back pocket. Don't leave your purse on a table and go to the restroom. Everywhere you went, it was your responsibility to keep an eye on your belongings at all times.

Even in your own home.

While I was living with my roommate in Bogotá, we bought a washer. My roommate's friend and I were in the kitchen, as two men delivered the washer into the room. My roommate was looking for the receipt, her friend had her back turned cutting vegetables, and I was left with the task of listening to the men explain, in Spanish, how the machine worked. Well, one of them left right after he dropped off the machine. I wondered why. As soon as both of the men left, my roommate's friend discovered the man who left first stole her phone off the top of the microwave. It was too late. They were gone. Just that quick. I was amazed that they would steal from us in our own home while we were in the same room.

I tried my best to stay quiet on public transportation and never speak English. My afro was my protector. They had no clue I was American until I opened my mouth. America symbolized wealth to them and they didn't associate it with blackness. This was the way of life, and tough for a suburban girl to get used to, especially since I was used to going to parties alone and leaving when I wanted to in my car. I didn't have my car and would have to be escorted at night, or I was taking my chances.

And that wasn't the only thing I had to adapt to. We got car bombed my first week there. It happened a few days after President Juan Manuel Santos was inaugurated. The day of his inauguration, I sat in the apartment with my new host family, hoping no one would bomb the city. I have this amazing instinct and that's the thought that had crossed my mind, even before it happened. It was the first time Colombia changed its Commander in Chief in eight years. And although I felt safe, I knew the FARC (The Revolutionary Armed Forces of Colombia, a guerrilla movement) still existed in Colombia. Everyone did. Many Colombians stayed in their homes; only those invited could attend the inauguration ceremony. So we waited, but magically nothing happened. Yet.

The Thursday after the inauguration, it occurred: August 12, 2010. I had no idea. I took the TransMilenio to work at La Universidad de La Sabana as usual. And then I noticed the professors talking and looking at the internet. They were saying something about a "carro bomba" and they had that same terrified look on their faces as my teachers did when 9/11 happened in the States. So I looked at the news outlets online and realized a car bomb had detonated around 5AM in front of the Caracol radio station in Bogotá's Chapinero neighborhood. The damage looked grave. Fortunately, I was staying about 100 blocks away from there, so I did not hear or feel the explosion. Looking at the reports, I knew I had to go there as soon as I got off work. My reporter instinct kicked in. I had to see it. I had to film it. I had to talk to people who lived through it. I wasn't working in news, but I had to go. So, I called my Colombian journalist friend, met him at the TransMilenio and he took me to the site.

I had never lived in a city where you had to worry about people bombing things, but my instinct told me it was going to happen sooner or later. There were guards with huge guns surrounding the damage. The Caracol radio station was destroyed. I soon learned that nine people were injured and taken to the hospital. Fortunately, no one died.

I internalized the fact that I was living in a country where guerrilla groups attempted to kill journalists for exposing the truth. The radio station was all caved in, with broken glass and concrete everywhere. Windows for blocks were broken on people's apartments. One woman who lived about a block and a half away said the bombing felt like an earthquake and it shook her out of her sleep. The news reports indicated someone drove a car up to the front of the radio station, left it and detonated the bomb. The Colombian government believed leftist guerrilla groups were responsible for the bombing, and that they did it to get the new administration's attention, letting them know the Civil War wasn't over. President Juan Manuel Santos responded by saying he thought it was a scare tactic and that he was not scared and would, in fact, continue to fight terrorism.

When I told my mom what happened, she freaked out and wanted me to come home. But for some reason, it didn't faze me; I told her I wasn't scared, and I wasn't coming home. Partially because I knew that wasn't all Colombia had to offer. And my thoughts proved true. Colombia was full of contrasts.

About a month into my stay, I traveled home to Ohio and back in a span of 36 hours. I was a bridesmaid in my cousin's wedding. When I returned, I went straight to the bank to get money out to pay rent. Inside, it was hot and the line was long. I hadn't eaten anything and suddenly, I felt dizzy. I decided to go to the ATM outside and complete multiple transactions to get out the money I needed. I passed out inside the ATM room and hit my head as I fell to the ground. Then I popped back up. Embarrassed, I ran out of the ATM onto the sidewalk and tried to walk home.

As I went to cross the street, a man was screaming, "Señora, señora."

I turned around, still out of it, and yelled, "What," in Spanish.

He then said, "tu tarjeta," or "your card." This kind man saw that I left my bank card on the ground near the ATM. I ran up to him and thanked him and retrieved my card. I then sat down and got some food from one of the food vendors nearby and waited until I had enough energy to try again getting the money out of the ATM. It was then I realized how the high altitude of Bogota must have gotten to me, having left and returned so quickly. But it also showed me early on there were some great people living in Colombia. Not everyone was out to rob and steal from the American. It was the first of the month. I had just gotten paid. If that man had kept my card, he could've had a lot of money. But instead, he did the right thing and I was forever appreciative of it.

Overall, during my first month there, I learned to be aware of my surroundings, to know the route to where I was staying and going at all times, and to avoid speaking English in crowded spaces. It just created unnecessary attention and you never knew who was listening.

Chapter 2:
Mi Casa Es Tu Casa

Colombia wasn't my first time living abroad. Two years prior, I had studied abroad for a semester in Santiago de los Caballeros in the Dominican Republic. My first time living outside the United States, my program decided to pair me with a host family, which I would highly recommend. Mine was amazing and I still consider them family to this day.

I was fortunate enough to live with a family that was all female—a mom and her daughter, who was a couple years older than me. I really felt a part of the family. I was 19 at the time so it was nice to have my host mom. She was a stay-at-home mom who cooked breakfast, lunch, and dinner, and washed my clothes. They didn't have a traditional washer over there and they hung clothes to dry, a practice I wasn't accustomed to.

The two-bedroom apartment we lived in was modest and about three blocks from the university. It was also close to "el Centro" or downtown Santiago and on a major public transportation route. The mother and daughter slept in one room and I slept in the other. We had an eating area and a living area, a computer desk, and one bathroom. Also, we often had to use the generator to shower, so I got about five minutes of hot water during my showers. Although mosquitoes were widespread in the Dominican Republic, I didn't have much of an issue with them in her apartment, so I didn't sleep with a mosquito net. I just put on my daily dose of bug spray and kept it moving. But, in many places in the Dominican Republic, it's recommended. Also, don't be surprised when you see the big cockroaches crawling around at night. Her home was immaculate and yet a few still managed to come out every now and then.

Her cooking allowed me to eat traditional Dominican meals daily and I loved it—food like plátanos and salami (plantains and salami), tostones (fried plantains), and mangú (boiled plantains). I loved how she stewed her chicken and her daily rice and beans. She learned my favorite meals quickly and would cook them all of the time. She also accommodated my numerous dietary restrictions; I'm lactose intolerant.

Additionally, through my host family, I got to participate in a traditional Dominican wedding at a cathedral, where they signed the wedding documents during the ceremony at the altar and also put this huge necklace around the couple. I also witnessed a very emotional memorial service my host mother orchestrated to remember her son, killed in a drunk driving accident, and her husband, who died from diabetes.

My host mother and I connected and we compared our two different worlds all of the time. We would chat for hours, often about the concurrent presidential elections happening in the Dominican Republic and the United States, and how Dominicans felt about race and Haitian relations.

I would question why often, when a dark-skinned black man appeared on the television, I'd hear, "¡Que feo!" or how ugly and every time the Mexican blonds appeared on the morning news, they'd say, "¡Que linda!" or how pretty. It was these exchanges and open dialogues that helped me better understand their culture, and helped them understand mine. Also, I believe providing my different perspective and having civil discourse may have changed how they thought about some things.

Despite our cultural differences, this was a woman who deeply cared for my well-being, would stay up-to-date on my school projects and dating life, and would tell me every time I left the house, "Qué te vaya bien con Dios (Go well and with God)." When the huge cockroaches would sometimes invade my private space as I returned home from a night out, she'd get out of bed and kill them for me. It wasn't an everyday thing, but sometimes they'd be there to greet me after a night of partying.

She was a host mom who let me live. After showing me how to get around, she realized I was good with directions and was independent. So, she didn't mind when I took trips with my friends around the country. She always knew where I was and who I was with, but she gave me a lot of freedom. And I handled it well.

I was living there before Skype and before adults were on Facebook. I had to use a calling card to speak to my family and it was very expensive. So I didn't. To get good internet service outside of the apartment, I had to pay to use computers at an internet café, which was also costly. So, my host family was all I had and they took great care of me. I've been back to visit two times and traveled across the United States to see them when they visited stateside.

If you're studying abroad in college, I definitely would recommend staying with a host family, and I hope your experience is similar to mine.

When I first arrived in Colombia, it was just the opposite. I was matched with a family of a mother and her adult children in a suburban neighborhood far from the hustle and bustle of Bogotá, but close to my job. It was a thirty-story apartment building and the family had a three-bedroom, two-bath apartment. The place had a tennis court and a pool. It was very nice, with tile floors and carpet. I had never seen carpet in Latin America, but I had only visited Puerto Rico and the Dominican Republic up until that point. The condo also had a fireplace. I had never seen a fireplace in a Latin American home either. The furniture was nice, as if it had come from the United States. I have to say, Colombians have nice furniture. The apartment was very modern, with a washer and dryer, and a balcony in my room. The woman had a maid who came more than once a week. She washed the clothes and ironed them and cleaned the house. There wasn't a dresser but instead an organizer in the closet. I noticed most Colombians had organizers in their closets.

The woman who lived in the apartment seemed kind of mean and strict. She wasn't down for me coming home late. Her two grown children were also living there, and all they did was work. No time for socializing with me, and they didn't seem interested in it either. There was nothing to do around there, nowhere that I could walk to. Then, one day, I came to the apartment and saw the maid on her hands and knees scrubbing the carpet, like she was Stanley Steemer. She was a mestizo woman. I assume that was the only work she could find. I didn't get a chance to speak to her as the woman of the house was steady giving her orders of what else to clean. I felt it was cruel. Yes, it was white carpet but it was already clean and I just felt so bad for that woman having to be on her hands and knees scrubbing the carpet with a rag. Apparently, she had to do that every week. And that's when I decided I had to leave that apartment. Once the dust settled from the car bomb, I moved on. It was just awkward and too sheltered. I had recently graduated from college and she had too many rules for me.

There was a website that proved to be very helpful, compartoapto.com. My friends told me to go on there and find an apartment and a roommate. It was basically a site that listed people who were renting rooms in their apartments and looking for roommates. It was what a lot of people used in Bogotá to find housing.

So I looked at a few and then I met Sofia*. She and her boyfriend picked me up and took me to her apartment. It was in a neighborhood called "La Castellana", much closer to the center of Bogotá but not too far from my job, which was in Chía in the northern suburbs of Bogotá. Her apartment was near a theater, hair salon, grocery store, and a few "centro commerciales" or malls, and it was within walking distance to the TransMilenio, my gateway to the rest of Bogotá. It was gated and had a security guard on duty 24/7. Having lived abroad before, I knew these were things that were important to me.

When she showed it to me, I liked it and I liked her. The place had white tile throughout, and a big living room with a fireplace. The bedroom was nicely furnished. She had a queen bed for me, and I had my own bathroom with a tile/glass shower. The kitchen was nice, as well. One of the downfalls though—it was a penthouse suite, meaning I had to walk up five flights of stairs daily. However, I liked it and it was in a strata four neighborhood.

There was a social class system in Colombia that they used when they charged people for their utilities. The system was designed so people living in the upper statuses (strata five and six) paid more for services like electricity, water and sewage than the groups in the lower strata. One was the lowest strata, where the super poor folks lived, and six was the highest strata, designated for the super-rich people. So I thought four was a happy medium for me because the rent skyrocketed once you lived in a strata five neighborhood.

Sofia was a sweetheart overall. She was hardly ever home and mostly at her boyfriend's house. That meant I had the four-bedroom apartment to myself most nights. While I had previously opposed hiring maids, after a few months of living in that huge apartment with white tile floors, I couldn't resist. I could not mop up those footprints every time I turned around. So I adapted to the culture. But I didn't believe in inhumane treatment. Sofia called a woman named "Martha" whom she had previously contracted with. She was an indigenous woman. She came once a month solely to mop the kitchen, living room, and bathroom floors, and to clean the bathrooms and kitchen. She usually only stayed for less than a half day and we paid her a full day's work. I was amazed to see that she cleaned better than I ever could.

Sofia and I had our ups and downs. She had a production company which made commercials for clients. On one occasion, she featured me in the commercial. But overall, we didn't talk much. She did speak great English, but for some reason we didn't go out together very often. She wasn't into salsa dancing or reggaeton like me. I guess we just came from two different worlds.

The issues that come with life don't stop just because you're living abroad. Soon after I moved in, I became frustrated because the roof in my bedroom kept leaking. This was a renovated apartment. We experienced a lot of rain and something was wrong with the roof. Talk about disappointment. Sofia had to work so I was left to communicate with the plumber in Spanish about the roof, and water leaking into my bedroom. I would come home and there'd be water all over the floor. Fortunately, it was happening by the window and not near my bed. But still, it was quite annoying. They kept doing patchwork instead of fixing the problem. It turned out the landlord lived in Mexico and the plumber was no help. I had to deal with the inconvenience on about five separate occasions. And the language barrier made it even more frustrating. That was a real turnoff. Eventually, Sofia ended up buying me a double bed and I moved into the other bedroom. She had extreme patience to deal with me on that one. The experience taught me how important it was to look at the structure of a building when I was considering moving into it, as well as how maintenance is handled. Again, I had just graduated from college, where I lived in college housing. This was my first time selecting housing on my own.

About halfway into my stay, we decided we wanted to cut our bills down, so she allowed her friend to move into my old bedroom. He was cool and he had his own bathroom so it didn't bother me too much, except for the crumbs he'd sometimes leave behind in the kitchen. But really the killer was when my roommate decided she wanted to couch surf. That meant allowing strange foreign men to crash at our place, without paying. That's when I about lost it. She just all of a sudden wanted to meet foreign people; I guess I wasn't good enough.

When these people came, they slept in the extra bedroom. Most of the time, I kept my door locked and stayed in my room when they were there. I often traveled on the weekends when they came. The first was an Australian. He arrived in February and kept saying ignorant things about the United States around me, such as how many foreigners hate Americans because we supposedly have an attitude that we are the best and come from the perfect country. He said we think that everyone wants to come and live in the United States. He tried to convince me that Australia was better because of its healthcare system. Then he tried to say Americans are stupid because we aren't worldly. It made me realize why 58 percent of Americans don't have passports, according to a Forbes.com article written by Niall McCarthy in 2018. Why leave the

USA to hear that nonsense? I told him the United States wasn't perfect, and there were plenty things to fix, but I couldn't think of a better place to live.

Then, he kept trying to come into my room and ask me what I was doing for the night, trying to insinuate I was going to go sleep with someone because in his mind, American women were easy and promiscuous. I felt very uncomfortable around him, but I didn't know how to tell Sofia because she knew I was against the entire concept. They were strangers and they weren't paying rent, and they were consuming our utilities. All she had to go on was these people's reputation on the couch surfing website—basically reviews from other people who they had stayed with.

What took the cake was when we were all eating breakfast, this fool picked up a green plantain and asked me, "Are the penises this big in America?" Talk about embarrassing and inappropriate. The stereotype he had about American girls was not me, nor did I ever feel comfortable talking about that to a complete stranger. Finally, Sofia chimed in and told him he was wrong and that behavior wouldn't be tolerated. After that, I told Sofia if she was going to have these people over, do it on the weekends when I was out of town because I couldn't stand it.
So that's what she did.

One time I came home to find this hippy-looking man, an American, who had hitchhiked to Colombia from California. He literally hitchhiked rides throughout Central America and came to Colombia from California on foot. No airplanes. Unbelievable, right? She allowed him to stay in our apartment. I just went to my room and locked the door. I was so frustrated that she would invite someone like that into our home. I recall he was super hairy and hadn't shaved and probably hadn't showered either. I left town the next day. There was also a guy from France. I don't remember much about him. So that was the gist of Sofia—all and all, a sweetheart who I try to keep in touch with even today.

One of my friends had a wild experience with her roommate that I believe is worth sharing because I wouldn't want it to happen to anyone else. She was renting a room in an apartment with a man who was gay. Of course there's nothing wrong with that but she had no idea what he spent his spare time doing. I presume they didn't talk much except for "hi" and "bye".

One evening, while she was in her bedroom with her boyfriend, she heard a young man in the hallway, screaming, "You didn't pay me for the sex! Pay me for the sex!" She told me on the phone that morning after it happened that the young man was holding a butcher knife and began to cut himself and the walls. She said blood was everywhere. When her roommate did nothing, she said the young man then came to her room. That's when her boyfriend stood between her and him, as he swung the bloody knife and continued cutting himself. She said he begged her to make her roommate pay for the sex. But my friend said she had no idea what the guy was talking about.

She got him out of her room and out of the apartment. But then things got worse. She said he went outside, found big rocks, and chucked them at the windows of the apartment, shattering glass everywhere. Long story short, her room and her apartment were completely destroyed. They called the police and my friend told me the police said they couldn't do anything because the young man was a minor. She asked her roommate what happened and her roommate first told her the young man was a pizza delivery guy who he let in the house and the man went crazy. Then, he admitted that he had sex with the boy and apparently didn't pay up. What I took away from it was it's better to pay more for rent in order to have armed security at the entrance of your apartment and know your roommates and what they're up to.

Stephanie Claytor

Chapter 3:
I Need A Ride

When I was living in the Dominican Republic, I learned about a lot of new forms of transportation. Remember, this was back in 2008 before Uber was invented. My host mother quickly introduced me to guaguas, conchos, and the Metro bus. That's because taxis existed but they were expensive to use for the everyday errands. Guaguas are usually vans in the Dominican Republic. There are public ones that often transport people throughout the city and to the countryside and rural towns in the mountains. There are private ones that can be rented. I rode in a private guagua with my classmates in my study abroad group, twice a month when we took a trip to a different city.

I rode the public guaguas often to visit the school where I was volunteering and when I went into the mountains to lead my girl's group. Usually, you can find the guaguas at the center of town and they often run all day long. Also, they're popular along the coast because they transport natives and tourists alike from one coastal city to another.

Rides in the guaguas are quite entertaining and a great way to learn about the culture. Often, the driver plays bachata music. There are usually about three or four rows of seats and the drivers try to pack as many people inside as possible. These vans are usually old with worn seats and the motor can often be heard while it's running. The fair is cheap and depends on the distance one is traveling. They have a city they commute between and they pick up and drop off people along the route.

I remember one time I rode with my classmate in a guagua from Puerto Plata to Cabarete. We were packed like sardines, sitting up against Dominican women who had just finished a day's work. The driver kept stopping along the road until the guagua was so packed that men were hanging out of the door, holding onto the side of the van. The bachata music was blaring and all of the women were singing along, as the coastal winds graced our faces. My classmate and I just smiled at each other, and prayed the men held on tight.

When I used to ride the guaguas to the mountains, it was a great time to get to know the locals. Since I rode up to the mountains every week, I began to see the same people riding in the van and I felt more comfortable talking to them. It usually wasn't as packed as other guaguas. Since there was a presidential election happening there in the

Dominican Republic, and President Barack Obama was running for office in the United States, we had plenty to talk about. Many of them told me they didn't believe the United States would elect a black man as president. I'd often ask them who they supported as president in their country. I enjoyed these conversations and it was good to hear from a variety of people about what they thought on these issues.

Rides in conchos were even more fun, because they are public cars. Imagine riding in a 1990s Corolla with six other people; that's a typical concho ride. The drivers kept stopping until they had four people riding in the back and three up front (two in the front seat). All while riding around in the Dominican heat with no air conditioning. Not exactly a comfortable ride, but definitely cheap and, for me, worth saving the money. Conchos were way cheaper than riding in a taxi. But, people on the tall or heavy side usually avoided them. You can imagine why. Sometimes the cars were missing a bottom, and you could see portions of the ground as you rode around.

The conchos ran on different routes, indicated by a letter in the window. They usually ran along the main roads throughout the city. Sometimes, to get across town, one had to catch multiple conchos. Fortunately, my host family lived on a concho route. To catch a ride, I would simply walk outside to the street and hold my thumb out to signal I wanted a ride. If the concho had room, they'd pull over and pick me up. Sometimes they'd cross three lanes of traffic to pull over to pick you up. Then you told them where you wanted to go, but it had to be along the route. If it wasn't, they'd tell you where to get dropped off and catch the next concho heading in that direction. To ride in the concho, you had to know how to speak Spanish and you had to know where you were going. I usually got my route confirmed before boarding. Since there were so many strangers entering and leaving, I usually never talked while riding in the concho, except to tell the driver "pare" or "stop" when I saw my destination. As a precaution, I only rode conchos during the day and I didn't carry valuables during these rides.

In the coastal areas and impoverished areas of Dominican Republic, there were moto conchos. These were motorcycles that acted like conchos and they could fit up to four people. I used to see entire families riding on moto conchos with plantains tied to the back. On one occasion, I rode one where I sat in the middle holding onto the driver's waist in front of me and my friend behind me. At first, I didn't want to ride on this stranger's motorcycle through the barrio, but then I realized that

24

was my only option, unless I wanted to walk for miles. I learned to do what I needed to do to get around. I sure didn't want to walk.

In Santo Domingo, they finally got a subway and I was able to ride it for the first time when I returned to the country in 2012. It was nice and, at that time, clean. I'm not sure what it looks like now; hopefully the same. It operated like any other subway in any other major city and was very helpful when it came to getting around that big city.

I also hitchhiked while living in the Dominican Republic. When the natives first suggested I do it, I looked at them like they were crazy. But, I quickly got with the program. It's the way of life there in the rural areas. When I went to the mountains between Santiago and Puerto Plata to volunteer every week, I took the guagua there, but the guagua stopped running after 5PM. There wasn't any published schedule. You just stood at the main road and waited for the guagua. If you stood there after 5PM and didn't see any guaguas coming by, well you stood on the side of the road with your thumb out, waiting for anyone to stop and give you a ride.

I never stayed overnight in the mountains outside Santiago. Most of the homes didn't have running water and barely any electricity. Also, there was only a colmado (corner store). In this area, I didn't see a real grocery store or restaurants or hotels. So, I always rushed to leave by 5PM to head back to the city, but sometimes people kept me after and I missed that last guagua back to the city. So, I flagged down a ride several times. It was normal for them but quite scary for me. I rode with the people until they got me off the mountain and back to the main street where I could catch a concho back to my apartment.

Once, I remember I ended up catching a ride with a man from the Rotary International. He was nice and he told me about all of the work they were doing in the country. But, on another occasion, I was terrified. I rode in the back of a dump truck with a nun and a Haitian man selling suckers. We all looked at each other and remained quiet until we got off of the mountain. During the ride, I peered inside the window at the drivers. They were young Dominican men, probably in their 20s, and it wasn't until we were winding around the hills that I discovered they were taking sips of rum. I just held onto the side of the truck and prayed. The nun was praying, too, because we all felt like we were going around those hills faster than normal. We made it to the bottom. I made sure I didn't stay in the mountains past 5PM after that.

When I arrived in the Dominican Republic, my study abroad teacher recommended we use her favorite taxi driver. I heeded her advice. I eventually came to know him as my driver. When I went out after dark, I called him to transport me and he was loyal.

It's safer to ride in a taxi at night and I'd recommend finding a driver you can trust and to get their number, so they can give you a ride whenever you need one. More than likely, your host family will not want to drive you around at all hours of the night.

One thing you will want to be cognizant of in the Dominican Republic is drinking and driving. When I was there, I didn't see DUI checkpoints like they have in the United States. People would often carry open bottles in their cars and drink alcohol while walking the streets. I never had this problem with people who drove as a profession. But it was an issue when accepting rides from friends. It's definitely something to watch out for.

Besides taxis, guaguas, conchos, and hitchhiking, the Dominican Republic also had buses similar to the Greyhound bus system. There were two main companies, "Metro" and "Caribe Tours". Caribe Tours was cheaper, but it was always freezing cold with the air conditioner blasting. The Metro was nice, but I usually took Caribe Tours because its schedule was more convenient. The buses offered rides between major Dominican cities. They were inexpensive and a great way to get around the country and usually on time. I enjoyed riding them and didn't feel unsafe.

I never drove in the Dominican Republic while I was studying there. When I returned in 2012, I rented my first rental car only because I wanted to travel across the country and it just seemed easier to have a car because I wanted to go places that weren't on the bus route. It was easy to drive to the coastal areas. Hardly anyone was on the highway and they were clearly marked. But driving through Santo Domingo was super treacherous! It was very difficult and my blood pressure skyrocketed because the guaguas and conchos would stop and cut across lanes at the drop of a dime to pick up passengers. Also, the motorcyclists weaved in and out of traffic. People did stop at traffic lights, but no one abided by the traffic lanes. It was chaotic. And there were huge chuckholes. Don't forget pedestrians and the numerous people knocking on your window trying to sell something at every light. Anyway, if you're going to the touristy coast areas, you'll probably be fine driving a rental, but if you're headed to Santo Domingo, be leery of driving unless you're used to driving in primarily urban areas.

While living in Bogotá, Colombia, I mostly rode the TransMilenio and took taxis at night. They had guaguas but they called them buses or busetas in Colombia. I only rode them to cities on the outskirts of Bogotá, such as Chia. Inside Bogotá, I avoided them because they were often crowded. I never drove in Bogotá and wouldn't recommend it. There were always "trancones" or traffic jams and the roads were very crowded and sometimes narrow. It was just much easier to ride the TransMilenio, take a taxi, or walk to wherever I wanted to go if the TransMilenio didn't go that route.

Colombia also had buses like the Greyhound, but the United States Embassy advised against using them, citing the current security environment. The Civil War in Colombia was mostly taking place in the countryside, outside of the country's major cities. The embassy also advised against driving or riding by road between major cities. The embassy's website advises road travel is especially dangerous at night because some roads aren't well-lit or maintained and some are prone to mudslides.

Also, in the countryside, livestock is herded along the road and since there aren't many sidewalks, pedestrians also use the roadway. Of course, I did both and I wouldn't recommend it. My roommate wanted to take a trip to Pereira. We never made it because we got halfway and there was a mudslide or something blocking the road. We sat for hours on the highway and then finally we turned around and went to another city, Honda. What I witnessed while riding the bus from Medellín to Bogotá overnight was some suspicious behavior that I'm too scared to put on paper. Take my word for it and just follow the embassy's warning.

Besides the TransMilenio, my main form of transportation in Colombia was by air. They had two Colombian airlines that I liked to use, Avianca and Aires. Aires was the cheap airline, but it got you where you needed to go. Avianca was more expensive but it always felt more comfortable and more professional. Since I had several American associates who were in the same program that lived all over Colombia, I used to travel every two weeks to visit them—a perk of only working on Tuesdays, Wednesdays, and Thursdays. One of the major advantages of living in Bogotá is it's in the center of the country so it's fairly cheap to travel to cities all over Colombia, usually $100 roundtrip. At least it was when I was there in 2010.

I often flew with Aires because it was more affordable. On many occasions, I got to my destination without any issues. However, there were a few times I experienced inconveniences. Once, I was in the airport waiting for my return trip to Bogotá from Cartagena. The crew said the Aires flight wasn't going to Bogotá that morning because of rain. So all of the Aires passengers were trying to get on the Avianca flight back to Bogotá, because like me, they all had to go to work. I had to literally throw my American passport into the worker's face to get a seat on that plane. There were very few seats available and lots of people in line waiting. On another occasion, I was in Cali and I got a phone call around 5AM the day I was supposed to head back to Bogotá, informing me that my flight had been moved up to around 8AM. I booked the flight purposely later in the morning so I could sleep in and have enough time to get to the airport. When I asked why, the woman on the phone with the airline told me something to the extent of the flight time was moved up because the other people on the plane wanted to return earlier. I had never heard of anything like that before. You never knew what you were going to get flying with them. They were cheap and they got me where I wanted to be, so for that I was grateful.

Traveling from Colombia to the United States by plane was a different story. I had to arrive at the airport two to three hours before my flight because the security checkpoints were numerous and intense. When obtaining the boarding pass, the workers took everything out of the travelers' carry-on luggage at the counter for everyone to see. They also thoroughly examined passports. I remember also seeing drug dogs walking back and forth constantly near the checkout counters. Then, the travelers went through a security screening similar to the United States. After passing that, the traveler headed to a boarding waiting room. But in order to enter that room, there was a long line. That's because each passenger boarding the plane had to have their carry-on luggage thoroughly examined. Security personnel again took out everything and put it on a table, examining every crack and crevice of the luggage or purse. Then, they patted down the passenger. While walking down the hallway to board the plane, there was another security team there, waiting to pat down each passenger. Again. Crazy, huh? It was all in the name of preventing cocaine from entering the United States, a process that was a part of the War on Drugs, I presume.

All in all, when it came to transportation, I loved to save money by taking conchos to get around the Dominican Republic and the TransMilenio to get around Bogotá. While it was best to take buses to travel around the Dominican Republic, it was safer to fly around Colombia. And finally, in both countries, it was best to get the number of a taxi driver I could trust and depend on who could transport me around at night.

Stephanie Claytor

Chapter 4:
What Do You Want To Eat?

When it came to the day-to-day living, Bogotá was similar to living in a big city in the United States. They had nice malls that were packed with people and food courts where one could get a quick bite to eat. I had high-speed internet in my home and access to Skype. FaceTime had just been invented, but no one really used it yet. I talked to my family on a regular basis. Grocery shopping was the same as in the United States, except I only bought what I could carry home since I didn't have a car and had to climb five flights of stairs with my groceries. I often found it was cheaper to buy my produce at the outdoor markets.

Colombia had a lot of its own brands. Anything American, such as Ocean Spray's Cran-Apple Juice, was really expensive. I recall it costing around $10 to $12. As a result, I adapted to the Colombian brands very quickly. On the other hand, generic foods were reasonably priced. In contrast to the Dominican Republic, in Colombia I had to cook my own food since I wasn't living with a host family. I cooked a lot of American foods, such as chicken wings and rice, burgers and French fries, and oatmeal. I ate out a lot, as well.

Colombians ate a lot of arepas or corn cakes, which I didn't like. A lot of their traditional meals involved milk, cheese or eggs, such as the bandeja paisa, which is a popular meal in Medellín that includes fried eggs, arepas, red beans, white rice, carne molida (ground meat), chicharron (fried pork rinds), plátanos maduros (sweet plantains), chorizo (spicy sausage), morcilla (a sausage filled with pig's blood, rice, onions, and spices), avocado, and lemon. I never ate this meal or many other traditional Colombian meals because I'm lactose intolerant and can't consume dairy or eggs. But, my friends always ordered it and loved it, although it's a lot of food.

Fortunately, in Bogotá, they had all of the American chain restaurants and most of the restaurants served American foods, such as steaks, burgers, and baked chicken. What I did love purchasing while I was out to eat were the drinks. Colombians make all of their juices fresh. So, while out to eat, you could get fresa (strawberry), maracuya (passion fruit), lulo, or guanabana juice. Each juice was blended with milk or water. Lulo looks like a small orange tomato and it has a citrus flavor. Guanabana had a flavor that was a combination of strawberry and pineapple with a hint of a sour citrus flavor. I usually preferred strawberry or maracuya juice, made with water, of course. On the Atlantic Coast, many of the restaurants offered limonada de coco or coconut lemonade, which tasted amazing.

In Colombia, my program advisors claimed the water was safe to drink and many people drank it. But after a few months of living there, I noticed my stomach would hurt after every meal and it'd send me to the bathroom. I never vomited, but I often wondered if it was the water that was upsetting my stomach. After a while, I started only drinking bottled water. So, drink the water at your own risk. Many people there will tell you the water is safe to drink but the Centers for Disease Control and Prevention advises against drinking tap water. You'll want to make sure the juices you purchase are made with bottled water, as well.

When it came to alcohol, Colombians loved Aguardiente. It means "fire water" and it looks like vodka, but it tasted more like licorice to me. It is made of aniz, which is a plant, and it is strong. People usually drink it straight. Aguardiente Antioqueño or the aguardiente from the Antioquia province, was my favorite. Antioquia is the province where the city of Medellín is located.

In contrast, in the Dominican Republic, they ate green plantains daily (tostones – fried, or mangú – boiled.) Mangú and salami was a delicious staple. They often had fruit for breakfast. Arroz y habichuelas (rice and beans) were a daily staple at dinner. And often my host mom would serve a stewed chicken for dinner, which was delicious. I loved her cooking. Dominicans also prepared a meal called "sancocho", which is a meat and vegetable stew usually comprised of pork sausage and chops, longaniza (Dominican sausage), butternut squash, chicken thighs, onion, green plantains, yucca, and corn accompanied with white rice and avocado. It takes hours to make but it is delicious! Another thing I noticed was that Dominicans were serious about not eating meat on Friday during Lent.

I didn't have to go grocery shopping often in the Dominican Republic, but when I visited the supermarkets, I saw that all of the food that wasn't Dominican was expensive. Rice, plantains, beer, rum and chicken were cheap. And that was about it. They had mostly American products, but they were expensive because they were imported. The major supermarkets were only in the major cities so many Dominicans had to travel quite a distance to access them. In their rural neighborhoods, they had colmados, which were like corner stores, that sold bread, water, rum, plantains, rice and beans mainly. They usually had bachata playing so you could get your groove on while you purchased these items—they were a hangout spot where people played dominoes, drank rum, and chatted.

Basically, in the Dominican Republic, drinking the water was a big no-no. You could use it to bathe and brush your teeth, but avoid swallowing it. Always ask for "botellas de agua" or bottled water. In most Dominican homes, they will have bottled water in the fridge for you to drink. When dining out, it's recommended to avoid eating from street vendors or food served at room temperature. Also, it's recommended to ask if the ice was made with tap water. If so, don't consume it. Also, you'll want to wash fruits and vegetables with bottled water. Always make sure you are drinking bottled water. It's something you'll have to be very vigilant about.

Overall, when it comes to food in Colombia and the Dominican Republic, my two main pointers would be never throw food away. You're expected to eat everything that's on your plate. Their philosophy is there are people starving so those who can afford to eat shouldn't waste it. If you're eating out and have allergies, always discuss it with the wait staff beforehand because many ingredients aren't listed on the menu in meal descriptions.

Stephanie Claytor

Chapter 5:
Access Denied

One thing that was stressful for me in Colombia was conducting business. Any type of business interaction seemed to be a hassle, whether it was something as simple as getting money out of an ATM or trying to rent an apartment. The banks seemed to make everything complicated. ATMs or cajeros were closed from 10PM to 6AM. Sometimes, they ran out of money. When I was there, I had to pay bills like lights, gas, internet water, etc. at the bank, between the hours of 7AM and 3PM on weekdays. Fortunately, I was off on Mondays and Fridays, but I don't know what the many people who worked five days a week did to get their bills paid. At the bank, there were always lines that were hours long. Of course, this was back in 2010. Maybe things have changed with online banking being so accessible elsewhere. Back then, I was only aware of being able to look at our account balances online.

Back then, I was told to rent an unfurnished apartment for a year or more, a considerable amount of paperwork was involved and required one-to-two cosigners who had property in Bogotá or around six months' rent in security deposits or advanced rent payments. This made it impossible for me to get my own apartment. The only other way would be to know someone and get them to fill out the paperwork in their name, which was not happening. So, I had to find a roommate and basically sublet. But, this was before Airbnb so things may have changed.

These are just a few reasons why I didn't want to live in Colombia long-term; it was too difficult to conduct business. I had to go to the cajero before 10PM. Although it seemed annoying at first, I guess it was a protective measure put in place so that if someone stole your debit card, they couldn't get any money out until the morning, which by that time, the victim would've already informed the bank. This was one of the many things we had to learn on our own through trial and error, reading the signs, and paying attention.

When it came to exchanging money, I got paid in pesos so I didn't have to exchange money often. I kept my American bank accounts open and I kept a little money in them, but I was mainly living on pesos, which involved mathematics.

I was also able to keep my American cell phone number. Verizon representatives helped me find a loophole in their policies that basically allowed me to suspend my service plan for $10 a month, however, I had to check my account every month and re-suspend or I'd get charged for a billing cycle. I used pre-paid phones while I was in Colombia and when I returned to the states, I called Verizon and my phone was back in operation again.

When it came to shopping, I noticed that in both Colombia and the Dominican Republic, clothing wasn't cheap. A lot of the clothing was imported. I stuck to the clothes I had and didn't buy too many new outfits. The majority of my budget was spent on transportation, entertainment, eating out, my phone bill, and traveling. For the most part, the cost of living in Bogotá seemed comparable to the United States. The only thing I recall being extremely cheaper was getting my hair, nails and toes done. I could get that all done in Bogotá for 25,000 pesos, which back then was around $12.50.

Everything was in the thousands of pesos in Colombia and 2,000 pesos seemed like a lot of money at first, but then when I went shopping and realized everything was priced in the tens and hundreds of thousands, I realized it all cost the same; the price tag just looked different. For instance, my rent was 800,000 pesos a month, which was $400 for my half. To help me convert the money, I always got rid of the last three zeros and divided the number by two. Eventually, I got used to the price of everything in pesos and I didn't have to convert as often. But, the exchange rate has changed since I've been there. It appears the dollar is worth more now than in 2010.

I'll say while living in Bogotá, I was amazed that the mall was super crowded. There were people and kids everywhere with full shopping bags. Back home, the malls were empty and dying after the recession. But in Bogotá, there wasn't room to breathe inside the mall. That's when I realized Colombia was a rich country. Everything there seemed to be expensive and mostly imported.

In the Dominican Republic, most of the price tags are in the hundreds and thousands. The exchange rates fluctuate constantly. The rate was different when I was there; the dollar was worth less. After a few months, I got used to the prices and cost of things and I didn't have to convert as much. It was inexpensive to live in the Dominican Republic. But, a lot of things were imported and those things were always expensive. Traveling and getting around was cheap. When I was living in the Dominican Republic, my study abroad group planned all of my vacations around the country so I didn't have to worry about that. I've since been back to visit and I'd say the resort rooms are similar to the price of rooms in the United States. Going out to eat, getting drinks, and the clubs were all affordable. Your money can go far there as long as you don't buy a lot of imported items.

It's also important to note that in the Dominican Republic, they refer to money as cuarto and in Colombia, they refer to money as plata. When it comes to adjusting to your new life abroad, it's important to learn the exchange rate quickly and what things generally cost, so you don't overspend. Dedicate time early on to visiting the stores and learning the prices of things. Negotiate with your phone company to find a cheap way to keep your American phone so you don't have to change your number when you return. Also, negotiate. Often abroad when you're buying from small business operators, you can talk them down in price for whatever you want to buy. That's probably the main skill I learned in the Dominican Republic; everything is up for negotiation.

Stephanie Claytor

Chapter 6:
The Lights Went Out

Something we take for granted in the United States and in countries similar to it is functioning utilities and how critical they are to our everyday lives. We have lights that we turn on and leave on even when we're not at home, wasting electricity. I learned in the Dominican Republic that many make do without it.

The Dominican Republic has serious issues with its electricity in rural and poor areas. I often went to visit my friend's family who lived in a poorer neighborhood in Santo Domingo. In their household, the electricity went out for several hours during the day, and several hours at night. You'd hear a loud, united chant throughout the barrio, "Se fue la luz". And that was when life stopped. It was mostly women left in the homes. They couldn't get much done without electricity. Most days, when "se fue la luz", we just sat around, drank a beer, and hung out until the lights came back on. At night, we held candles. I once tried to apply eyeliner and it was darn near impossible to hold the candle and the mirror to apply it. But they were pros.

Not having electricity wasn't an excuse for not having your makeup on for a night of fun. If you tried to get your hair done, sometimes they wouldn't be able to help you either if the lights went out. They'd offer to put your hair in rollers and let you leave the salon with them in to air dry and tell you to come back when the lights came back on so they could finish styling your hair. Another funny episode was when I was staying with a friend in Cabarete. It was in the evening and the lights were out. I had to go to the bathroom. It was so challenging to hold a flashlight while trying to hold my pants and squat to use the toilet. Then, I felt something crawling on me. I couldn't see what it was but I felt like it was crawling up my leg. I feared it was a cockroach, coming for me; my worst fear. I panicked and ran out of the bathroom screaming about the cockroach coming to get me. I just held it until daytime after that.

Contrarily, in my host family's home, I believe the lights went out sometimes as well, but I didn't notice because they had a generator. Many of the homes in the nice neighborhoods and the universities had them. In the poor households, they just went without.

Also, while visiting friends in Santo Domingo, there wasn't running water. Before visiting them, I had always taken running hot water for granted. But in the Dominican Republic, I realized how important running water and hot water were to my sanity. It was the first thing I ran to when I returned home. In these homes in the poorer neighborhoods in Santo Domingo, there was a huge barrel in the bathrooms and a pitcher. They would fetch water from the well underground and pour it into the barrel. To bathe, you'd stand in the shower area, rub the soap all over your body, and put water in the pitcher and pour it over yourself. The water was ice cold; it would send chills up and down your body. They mastered this and even did it when the lights went out. I, on the other hand, dreaded it.

The water was so cold it was like taking an ice bath. It's important to note that you'll have to bring your own washcloths because they don't use them much there; they use their hands and soap to bathe. At my host family's apartment, they had running water and a normal shower, except the hot water only lasted five minutes in the shower. I learned to take really quick showers. In the resorts, this was never a problem. The resorts had running hot water and constant electricity. If you're staying in a hostel, you'll definitely want to verify if they have hot water and a generator.

Air conditioning was also spotty. I personally don't like air conditioning, so it didn't bother me much. Again, the resorts had it but most of the homes do not, or they don't use it. But they usually have patios or just leave the doors open so there's always a breeze running through the home. At my university, they had window units and I hated it. They always had the air on and it was unbearably cold. A lot of the stores and clubs had air conditioning, too.

In Colombia, electricity wasn't an issue, at least not in the cities. The lights never went out there and everywhere I went had running water. It was similar to the United States. As a matter of fact, my shower in Bogotá was the best shower I'd ever had. It was tiled all around and it had a glass wall and a huge shower head. In our apartment, hot water didn't come out of the faucets and showers unless you turned on the hot water heater. To turn it on, I had to plug it in, turn on the gas, and flip a switch. The calentador or hot water heater was in the kitchen so this was a painless task. I could also set the temperature. You better believe I always turned it up for my steaming-hot showers. Compared to the Dominican Republic, this was heaven. I believe I upset a Colombian once. They asked me what I liked about Colombia the most and I said my hot showers. They just didn't understand.

In Bogotá, it was around 60 degrees during the day and perhaps 40 degrees at night, every day. There was no need for air conditioning. But we also didn't have heat. So with the tiled floors in my apartment, I was freezing at night and always wearing sweats. That's why those hot showers were so amazing. After the sun went down, it was always cold outside. I'd often have to walk from the TransMilenio to my cold apartment. That's another reason why those hot showers were so important. So when picking an apartment in Bogotá, make sure it has steaming hot water capability.

I didn't mind that hot water didn't come out of the sinks naturally. I saw it as conserving energy and I thought it was quite progressive. We don't need hot water to brush our teeth.

Most of the people in Colombia had a washer but they didn't have clothes dryers. They hung their clothes to dry inside their homes. Since Bogotá's weather was fall/spring weather year-round, it was usually kind of cold to dry clothes, so you had to take advantage of the few sunny, warmer days. Otherwise, your clothes would be hanging to dry for two to three days.

To pay for these utilities, Bogotá had a unique system where it divided its neighborhoods into strata—0 equaled abysmal poverty or homeless and 6 signified wealthy. The Calle 100 area in Bogotá was classified as a 6. Where I lived was stratum 4: middle class. Below stratum 3 started to look impoverished and the services, such as electricity, were less dependable. The sad thing was people learned their stratum or place in Colombia very early and many times they never escaped it. They knew the strata of the different neighborhoods and often didn't venture into neighborhoods outside of their class. Many of the rich neighborhoods weren't accessible to public transportation and I believe that was by design. Most of the rich Colombians had cars so it didn't matter to them. The system was designed to alleviate urban inequality by allowing the poor to pay less for their utilities. The strata was based off of the home's characteristics, not a person's income. But in the lower strata, poor housing often correlated to poor families. In my experience, it led to prejudice and stigma and social segregation. It divided the social classes even more and it sometimes made it difficult for people in stratum 1 and 2 to get good jobs. When people mentioned where they lived, it was easy to identify what stratum they lived in and they were often judged by it.

So what I learned from this experience was not to judge people by their stratum. I met some wonderful, intelligent people who lived in stratum 1 and 2. When it came to housing, it was important to understand this stratification system before selecting where I wanted to live. If my friends hadn't informed me, I would've probably been living in stratum 5 and been paying higher utility bills for no reason. My home in stratum 4 was perfectly fine.

Chapter 7:
All Spanish Isn't the Same

Spanish is a very diverse language with a gazillion dialects, just like English and French. It seems like each country has its own take on how to speak Spanish, and then different regions within the country also speak the language differently, especially in Colombia. I figured this out early on when I was taking high school Spanish classes and getting straight A's, and then I'd go to the Mexican restaurant and couldn't understand a word they were saying.

It's essential to have a basic understanding of Spanish and basic words for simple things like car, truck, spoon, knife, home, room, etc. Everyone will understand you, but they may not use those words in return. Also, it's good to understand how to form sentences and how to conjugate verbs. That's where Spanish class comes in handy. Once you have that foundation, it's all about learning new vocabulary and using it. I would suggest learning the vocabulary of the place you're moving to; watch their shows and read their news. I guarantee they will use different phrases and verbs from what you have learned in a Spanish class offered in the United States.

Colombian Spanish differed from everything I was taught. Every region had its own distinct dialect. Medellín's people, referred to as "paisas", had their own way of speaking, people from Cali had their own dialect, and the costeños or people from the coast had a Caribbean way of speaking, similar to Cubans, Dominicans, and Puerto Ricans. They were more direct and they chopped off their words, as well as refused to annunciate the syllables. Because I was used to this Spanish, I preferred it.

Bogotános, on the other hand, were quite challenging to understand. They spoke in a very formal manner, using Señora and Señor to direct their attention to someone, instead of in the Dominican Republic, where everyone was "amiga" or "amigo". When people from Bogotá received a service, they said "gracias, muy amable" or "thank you, you are very kind". My problem with that was the person was simply doing their job so I didn't understand why I had to emphasize how kind they were. It seemed extra to me. Also, when they asked for a service, they said "por favor", "regálame" or "puede regalarme", which literally meant "can you gift me", instead of "can I have this or that". In my opinion, because this was everyday custom, the true meaning of those words was lost.

In addition, they would take a basic word and find the most advanced synonym and use that, instead of the basic word. It was as if they talked like they wrote. So, I realized that my Spanish was not horrible; it was just that they were using a whole new vocabulary that I had to learn. And when I refused to adapt to some of their formal ways, some thought I was rude when really I was just being direct, cutting to the chase. I refused to say five sentences to get one point across. I guess that was just me. Some of their most used phrases included:

- "Qué pena" – what a shame (for you). This was often said when they did something wrong that affected you. They didn't say "lo siento" or "I'm sorry" but instead usually said "Qué pena".
- "O sea" – I mean
- "Averiguar" – figure out or inquire – they love this verb and often use it when trying to set up something, such as a meeting or date.
- "Marica" – a gay person, or dude/friend, – for some reason and I never understood this, my college students used to call everyone this. They'd say "ay marica" this and "ay marica" that. I guess it has lost its meaning.
- "Parce/parcero" – friend
- "Bacano" – something that brings happiness, cool
- "Qué chimba" – something that produces happiness or is cool
- "Filo" – hungry, the same as saying "tengo hambre" or "I'm hungry"
- "Camello" – job
- "Una fria or pola" – beer
- "Rumbearse" – to go party all night without commitment

In contrast, Dominican Spanish was at the opposite end of the spectrum. They would cut off the endings of words and cut to the chase when speaking. Their Spanish was informal and they didn't use too many advanced words, at least the majority of people I came across. I just had to keep up with their speed and their slang. To me, it often felt like Spanish "chopped and screwed", similar to down south music.

For instance, instead of asking "Como estas" or "how are you", they would ask, "Como tu 'ta?" The ta coming from the end of estas. And tu in Spanish means you. Another popular phrase was "vamos p'allá", which in formal Spanish is "vamos para allá" or "we're going over there," cutting off the "ara" in para. Some of their most popular phrases include:

- "Qué lo que" – What's up
- "Tato" – that's cool, also used to say alright or bye
- "Oye" – listen, you heard that
- "Mira" – look
- "Vaina" – thing (used for everything. I said it every time I didn't know what the word for it was and pointed to it. For example, "Esa vaina no funciona" or "That thing doesn't work.")
- "Chévere" – awesome, cool
- "Chin" – a little bit, such as "dame un chin" or give me a little
- "Tiguerona or tigre" – a street corner hustler or street-smart person

There's a ton of other Dominican slang out there. I suggest brushing up on it if you're headed to live in the area. However, the Spanish there was much easier to adapt to and understand than it was for me in Colombia. Your vocabulary will expand more in Colombia than it will in the Dominican Republic, for sure.

It's also important to note that many Spanish speakers understand English; they just can't speak it. I learned that the hard way while visiting my friend's family in Puerto Rico while I was in college. We were trying to leave her grandmother's home to go on a date at the movies with some boys we met.

Her grandmother had a gate with a lock on it that we had to undo to get out of the house. My friend was telling me in English the game plan for how we were going to get out. Before she finished, her grandmother came into the room and said, "Come here." She then proceeded to chew my friend out and tell her we weren't going anywhere and to give her back the key. She even threatened to kick us out. And we still had five days left on vacation staying at her home. My friend came back into the room and told me what happened and she was pissed! That's when I learned my lesson—to avoid assuming people didn't understand English just because they couldn't or refused to speak it.

My top tips for learning the language would be to learn idioms for the country you're moving to, find someone from that country that you can speak to often so you can learn their dialect, and when speaking Spanish, it's also important to know where the other person in the conversation is from. A good example of why this is important is the word "coger". Dominicans use the word often when asking someone to take, get, or pick up something. But to Mexicans, coger means to have sex. So to avoid embarrassment, learn the differences in each Spanish-speaking region.

Chapter 8:
Do You Speak English?

The purpose of my stay in Colombia was to teach English to college students at La Universidad de La Sabana. Colombia desperately needed native English speakers, so I got paid simply because I was a native English speaker. But I took my job more seriously than that. I was there to teach them about American culture; I preferred to teach them about African-American culture—a rare treat my students would have probably never encountered had I not been their teacher.

During my English conversation club sessions, my students learned about black culture. One week, they watched a movie about President Obama's campaign trail. The next, they watched a Lester Holt documentary about the Civil Rights movement. I even made them watch *Soul Food*.

One day, I wanted to make sure they understood the difference between American English dialects. We did an exercise where I played music videos from different genres of music: Gospel, R&B, Rap, Country, and Pop. They had to listen to the songs and decipher what was being said, and the meaning of the songs. They did fine deciphering what was said in the R&B, Gospel, Pop and Country songs, but when I played Lil Boosie's hit "Independent", their heads were spinning. They looked confused as if they were hearing another language besides English. I had to play the song about five times before they had an idea of what the song was talking about. The moral of that lesson was American English has many dialects, and they needed to get hip if they wanted to be successful in los Estados Unidos.

I probably had the most fun teaching the conversation club. I led those sessions once a week. When I wasn't doing that, I conducted English placement tests. All of the incoming students were tested on their English skills. They needed to be able to speak, read, and write in English in order to graduate from college.

Some of the students did very well; most of them had family in the States. But there were some who came to see me in a three-piece suit and couldn't speak a lick of English. It was as if their dressing skills were supposed to overcompensate for their lack of English.

I learned a lot about English language learners. In Spanish, sentences often go on and on. A lot of the incoming students wrote passages, and they never used a period, just commas. It was as if a period didn't exist. That drove me nuts. Also, what separated the good English speakers from the bad was their vocabulary. If they couldn't answer my questions or if their answers didn't make sense, they were put in lower-level classes. I placed very few in upper level classes.

When I wasn't doing all of that, I substituted classes and gave presentations about America. For the most part, the students were respectful. One time, the students tried to confuse me to get out of class early; I outsmarted them. There was a "huelga" or strike for the truck drivers on the highway in front of the school. The students tried to trick me and tell me that class was canceled because the highway was going to close soon due to the huelga. I said, "Now wait a minute. No one has notified me that class is canceled. So until then, everyone will remain in this classroom and learn English." I made a phone call and confirmed class was not canceled. The students tried to trick me, but I was not the one. By the way, the huelga did happen, but they didn't shut down the highway. Everyone made it home safely.

I guess I was such an excellent teacher that by the second semester, they gave me my own class—Level 4 English, the intermediates. I had a handful of students. We had to complete the exercises in the book and they were given weekly exams. My number one rule was to use English when speaking to me.

They would come up to me and say, "Teacher, no pude hacer mi tarea porque", and before they could finish, I'd say, "English". First you're giving me an excuse why you didn't do your homework, and then you have the nerve to whine to me in Spanish about it in my English class. I was not having that. At least have the decency to tell me your excuse in English. Zero it is for you. I was strict. Heck, the kids were as big as me and some the same age. That was the only way I was going to get respect there. But for the most part, the students were well-behaved.

When I wasn't teaching, I had the opportunity to host my own radio show, with my girl Rosanelle. She was another English teaching assistant from Barbados. We had a fun time. The college had a radio station and they wanted one of the shows to be in English. It was actually cool. Every week, I would write the show and select the music to prepare for it. I would interview the exchange students from around the world that were studying at the university, and then make the show about their country of origin. So, I'd play music that was topping the charts in their country and talk about the news going on over there. Then, I'd interview the student about their hometown, why they came to Colombia, what they thought of it, what they liked, disliked, etc. I really enjoyed it. I interviewed people in English from South Korea, China, Canada, Venezuela, Brazil, Tunisia, Belgium, Great Britain, Australia, and Norway.

Universidad de La Sabana was located about 30 minutes north of Bogotá in a town called Chía. Every day I had to ride 40 minutes to work and catch two buses. It was surrounded by canals, which later were its downfall. My teaching there ended when the university got flooded around Easter and they told me the semester was over, and there was no need to come back because the place was under water. It wasn't surprising considering it rained there every day at 4PM. It was a beautiful campus, though, with brick buildings and open air. It had a country feel.

The university was something else, though. It was where the rich kids went, and it was known for its communications school. They offered some scholarships. I didn't see many Afro-Colombian students there; Rosanelle and I stood out like sore thumbs.

This was Colombia and yet I'd see kids roll up in their Abercrombie & Fitch shirts, and leave in their own cars—Benz, you name it. I'd sit and think, *Where is all of this money coming from*? Walking around there, Colombia definitely seemed like the United States, and not the poor third-world country they make it out to be on the news in the States. And forget being friendly. Every day I'd go to lunch and sit at a table and no one would sit with me, or even talk to me. It was as if I didn't exist. If Rosanelle didn't have lunch at the same time, I usually ate by myself. I guess that's what happens when you have an afro sitting on top of your head. In Colombia, you were supposed to straighten your hair and wear makeup. I did neither.

During my time there, I had two students who left a mark. One, Veronica, who actually came and visited me in the United States, a few years after I left. She was Afro-Colombian and a nursing student from Cali. She attended a few of my English Conversation Club sessions, but wasn't in any of my classes. I was very inspired by her English-speaking abilities. She was about two years younger than me, but I didn't get to hang out with her much outside of school because she lived in south Bogotá, about a two-hour ride on the TransMilenio from where I lived. One day, she invited me to try out for an African dance troupe she was in. I made the two-hour trek to the unknown side of Bogotá where Americans didn't dare to visit. She picked me up in El Centro and accompanied me to the Southside.

That was a workout I'll never forget. It was a room full of Afro-Colombians in this tiny one-room house. I forgot to bring a water bottle. My mistake. I thought we were just going to dance like in college. No problem? No. The leader of that troupe damn near killed me. He made us do these African dances where we were shaking literally every bone and piece of fat in our bodies, popping this way and that. We'd dance for like 30 seconds, and then pause for a second and get back in line and do it again. No breaks. An hour or two later, "Ooh child." My ribs felt like they were going to crack from all of that popping. I learned I was out of shape. When I left, I knew I probably wouldn't make that dance team, but I was glad Veronica invited me to have the experience.

The other student that made an impact was Camilo. He had curly hair and didn't wear the Abercrombie & Fitch clothes like the rest of the students. I guess that's why I was his favorite teacher, another outsider. One day, I was feeling sick with what Colombians would refer to as gastritis. I think it was the cafeteria food that made my stomach growl. Anyway, I was in a lot of pain and I told Camilo. He said he'd help me go to the clinic, which was connected to the university. So we walked there and he made sure I didn't pass out. When we got there, he talked to the nurses, and then I went into the exam room alone.

Boy, was that fun—explaining my medical issues and pain in Spanish to the doctor. The doctor was looking at me like I was crazy. I mean, I could speak Spanish, but I never took a class on medical terminology. And I had never been sick, especially in Latin America. There was never a need for me to go to the doctor; this was a pain I had never had before. I probably couldn't have explained it in English properly, which made the situation worse.

I kept telling her, "Esta vaina me duele (this thing hurts)," pointing to an organ near my stomach. I had no idea what it was in English and had no idea of the word in Spanish. It could've been my pancreas, abdomen, who knows. She just looked at me and tried to understand. She gave me some pills to take that eventually helped. She said I had "gastritis", which it seemed every Colombian had. Looking back, it probably was the water that they said was drinkable but probably wasn't because after living there for a while, I kept getting the bubbles after everything I ate. Needless to say, Camilo was there for me during a worrisome time. Thank God it wasn't anything worse.

When trying to get a teaching job overseas, I'd suggest looking for programs that are already established because they will have everything set up. The United States has the Fulbright English Teaching Assistantship program, which has spots in most, if not all of the Latin American countries, and around the world. The requirements for each country are different but the participating Latin American countries all require language proficiency. For this program, they like to select people right out of college, but it's unique because you only have to teach 20-30 hours per week and then complete a social or community project on the side. They give you a stipend to live off of, as well. I've had friends who have also received teaching opportunities fairly easily in Cartagena. Also, the University of Sabana loved native English speakers. You could always contact the college directly and apply to teach or become a professor.

Stephanie Claytor

Chapter 9:
Student Life

Before I was a teacher in Colombia, I was a student in the Dominican Republic. I attended college at Pontificia Universidad Católica Madre y Maestra (PUCMM) in Santiago de los Caballeros or Santiago for short. I loved being a student there. As my dad put it, I wasn't studying but rather on a four-month vacation. I'd have to agree. I learned far more on the streets than I did in the classroom, but my classes were fun and useful, too.

At the university, we mostly attended classes in a separate building with the Haitian students. They called it the international building. Our classes were taught in Spanish but sometimes the teachers spoke English. The workload was easy. We had tests every so often and essays for homework, in addition to light book reading and heavy classroom discussions. I took classes on gender studies, Dominican-Haitian Relations, Spanish Grammar, Spanish Literature, and Community Involvement. The majority of my classes had all American students, except for my Dominican-Haitian Relations class. That class had Haitians, Dominicans, and Americans and was always entertaining.

Usually, all of the American students were in the computer lab after class doing our homework together. We rarely had a reason to walk around the sprawling campus because all of our classes were mostly in one building, at the entrance of the university. We usually took a few classes in the morning and then returned home for lunch.

A lot of the college students hung out at bars nearby and we'd hang out there with them. Also, a lot of us hung out with the Haitian students because they spoke more English and liked a lot of American music, such as Hip Hop. They'd host parties at their apartments and invite us. The Haitian students that went to PUCMM were from wealthy families and usually spoke four languages: Haitian Creole, French, English, and Spanish.

PUCMM had a lot of American students studying there from various colleges across the United States. There were about 50 of us on campus so we never felt lonely. My program was a small program offered by the liberal arts colleges in Upstate New York, but the Council on International Educational Exchange had a huge contingent of American students studying there since they have a well-established program.

My program was awesome! There were about ten of us and our

program included many educational vacations every other weekend. So, we got to know each other very well. We would ride in a guagua with our Dominican program director and our driver all around the island. We visited the home of one of the Mirabal Sisters, who were well-known for being outspoken against Dictator Rafael Trujillo. We went to Samaná and learned about the African-American descendants living there. We visited the free trade markets in Dajabón and crossed the border into Haiti. We took a tour of the capital, Santo Domingo. We visited the Larimar mines in the southwest corner of the country. Larimar is a beautiful blue stone that can only be found in the Dominican Republic. We also stayed in a resort in Punta Cana. The trips were very informational and probably what I remember the most about living in the country. If you're looking to study there or any other country, I'd recommend finding a program that has this traveling component; seeing the country for yourself and talking to the living legends is much more memorable than reading about it in a book.

Chapter 10:
Get Involved

I was involved in several community service projects in the Dominican Republic. One of the projects consisted of riding to the campo or countryside every week to lead a girls' group. I adored these young women. The girls' club was a program the Mother's Wish Foundation founded in a rural community in the mountains between Santiago and Puerto Plata. The girls were between the ages of 13 and 18. My goal was to start a project with them, which eventually became making commercials about their dream jobs. First, I had to get them to discuss what they wanted to be. At 13 years old, most didn't have a clue because I guess they figured adult life for them meant marrying at 18, having kids, and depending on a man for the rest of their lives. That appeared to be life in the campo. Finally, most said they either wanted to be doctors or work in tourism. I made them write essays about their goals in life. Many of them had difficulties writing in Spanish, so I worked with them to correct their essays. Before I left, they all participated in making their own videos where they talked about their career goals and we had an end-of-semester party. We had a ton of fun and it was a very memorable experience.

Back then, there wasn't Facebook so I wasn't able to stay in touch with the girls to see if they followed through. I did return to the rural village about four years later and learned that some of the girls were married with kids.

I loved going up to this campo because I'd hang out with people in the community after I finished my girls' club sessions. I met a black family, meaning a darker-skinned Dominican family. The woman was hilarious! Her name was Rosa. She had about three rooms in her wooden frame house and five kids. She had this deep, raspy voice that reminded me of black women from back home. She always served me café and we would sit and talk outside, while she smoked her cigarette. I interviewed her for my black beauty project. During the interview, she tried to get me to marry her son. When I returned to visit in 2009, she took me around to get "the number" (lottery number) from the neighbors. I played and told her she could keep the money if I won. During that visit, she told me her son got tired of waiting and married someone else in the neighborhood.

Along with the girls' club, I taught once a week at one of the elementary schools that had a name too long to pronounce. I was supposed to teach them English but in the third grade classroom, some of the students didn't know the Spanish alphabet so I had to teach them Spanish first. We worked on basic phrases and reading sentences and writing new vocabulary words. Imagine me just learning Spanish and trying to teach them. It worked out though.

They were reading better and better by the time I left. I was assigned to tutor about three boys and one girl, set aside in a room next to the principal's office, a short friendly woman. One day, one of the boys named Henry inappropriately touched my ribs under my arm. He was nine. I jumped and looked at him and told him to go sit down across the room. What do you do in a situation like that? He was trying to test me. At nine years old. He never did it again. I guess the look on my face told him it was inappropriate. It just made me feel awkward, like I didn't want to be stuck in this room with these troubled kids.

One day, the kids I was tutoring pissed me off so bad I asked them if they wanted to be concho drivers for the rest of their lives, and if not, they'd better listen to me and focus on their schoolwork. After that, they started paying attention. Now this was a public school, meaning a lot of the low-income kids attended. When the teachers didn't show up for work, there wasn't a substitute; the principal had to take over.

So, a couple of times, I showed up to volunteer and she gave me entire classrooms to teach because the teacher just didn't show up for work. (I believe they were underpaid). It was hilarious because once I was given a fourth-grade classroom and the kids didn't believe I was from the United States or that I could speak English. Because when I was there, I never spoke a lick of English. One of the students had the nerve to ask me to count to 20. I did it like we used to in elementary school, really fast. Her eyes got as big as quarters. The child was in disbelief. I asked her what she thought.

She thought I was Dominican because she said, "Tu no eres rubia".

And I said, "Not all Americans are rubia. Do you know Beyoncé? She is American and she isn't rubia."

I was explaining to her that not all Americans are white with blond hair. The class looked at me dumbfounded.

In Colombia, my community involvement wasn't as structured. My goal was to use my spare time to create a documentary about Afro-Colombian culture. I somewhat succeeded. While I traveled around the country, I brought my video camera with me and always set up interviews to speak to people from various spectrums of the community. I went to Quibdó, one of the predominantly black cities in the Chocó province and spoke to leaders there about life. I then put my video about Quibdó on YouTube. I also got a press pass to film the World Salsa Festival in Cali, Colombia.

In Bogotá, I visited "La Familia Ayara," a cultural center that offered classes on rap and Hip Hop. It was run by Don Popo Ayara, who in 2018, eight years later, was running for senator. Back when I visited, this was where aspiring rappers met and perfected their craft. I went to one of the shows and it was awesome to see the raw talent displayed there. It was a way out for these kids living in poverty—a place where those kids could express what was happening in their lives and the struggles they endured.

Also, I visited San Basilio de Palenque and talked to young leaders there about the town, which is known as the first freed slave town in the Americas. I also returned there with my friends to teach teen girls there about family planning and self-respect. This town was very rural and very poor. We worked with a Colombian nurse to offer that informative session. I'll never forget the nurse demonstrating how to put on a condom using my tripod. Participating in these educational visits and giving back just made my time in these countries so much more purposeful. It created memories I'll cherish forever. Going off the beaten path and creating my own experiences was so worth it.

I'll also never forget the time Angela Davis came to speak to students at one of Colombia's most liberal colleges, La Universidad Nacional in Bogotá. It's an experience I blogged about and remember vividly. During my second month living in Bogotá, American prison abolitionist and black feminist Angela Davis, visited the prominent Universidad Nacional to discuss America's prison industrial complex. She spoke before a crowd of more than a thousand people. Before her speech, she met with students on campus and visited women's jails around Colombia.

"When I visit a country, I always visit the jails to learn about state violence and how they treat the extreme members of society," said Angela Davis during her discourse.

What was striking to me as a black American was the tenacity to which Bogotános, including whites, blacks, indigenous, and mestizos, fought for more than a half an hour, banging on the doors of the closed auditorium, to get a chance to see her. This was not the case at Syracuse University, where I heard her speak before. But from a Colombian perspective, this was not surprising. La Universidad Nacional was one of the most liberal institutions I'd ever visited. There were graffiti signs on campus buildings against the U.S. military, and revolutionary guerilla leader Che Guevara's face painted above the auditorium entrance.

After everyone was allowed entry, and half the crowd had their translating machines, the encapuchados or hooded ones, a leftist revolutionary student group, came running onto the stage from below in the middle of Davis' introduction. They had everything covered, concealing their identities. As they took over the microphone, the audience began to chant with them, as if this was a normal occurrence. For those who were not students or faculty at La Universidad Nacional, it appeared that Davis was going to get kidnapped. And by the look on her face, especially since she was not fluent in Spanish, it was appeared she thought so, too.

Then the group raised the Black Panther Party flag and the Pan African flag, and the audience let out a sigh of relief along with Davis; the group was not there to cause harm. After they spread their message about living in a freer society, Angela Davis finally took the podium. She began her discourse by reminding the audience that October 13th marked the 40th anniversary of her own arrest for fraud, murder, kidnapping, and conspiracy. It was this imprisonment that forced her to fight for those imprisoned worldwide. She thanked those at La Universidad Nacional who fought in the worldwide movement to free her and acquit her of the accused crimes.

Davis' message to Colombians was very clear: prevent the American Industrial Prison Complex from being replicated in Colombia. She explained to the audience that the industrial prison complex was a system where capitalism and the government benefited from having numerous prisons full of people that the middle and upper echelon of society did not want walking the streets, such as the poor and minorities. According to Davis, the industrial prison complex was a remnant of slavery, but instead of slave masters, companies such as those in the medical, telecommunications, retail and construction industries profited off of those incarcerated and had a major incentive to lobby to continue to incarcerate thousands of people. She explained why so many living in poor, Black, and Latino communities were imprisoned in the United States. She blamed it on police hyper-surveillance of these communities, making it easier to find these members of society committing a crime. Davis said she supported the closure of all of United States' prisons. In her opinion, the system wasn't fair because the poor and people of color were sent to prison at a higher rate than whites and the rich, who committed the same crimes.

"Race determines who goes to prison and who doesn't," Davis declared during her talk.

Instead of incarcerating people, Davis said the American government needed better education and health systems. She claimed it needed to offer more services to the poor. She believed that this, with less vigilance in black and Latino communities would lead to the reduction of crime.

"We need a new society, not based on profit, but on serving human beings," said Davis. "We need to unite our hearts and struggle for a better world."

After describing the American system and its incentives, she explained how it related to Colombia. She told the crowd there that more than 75,000 Colombians were imprisoned, and according to Davis, there were agreements between the Colombian and the United States government to construct more prisons in Colombia with the capacity to hold thousands more inmates.

As a young, African-American woman, her speech struck me. I was glad she shared this American reality with the Colombian people. It's a reality that many young black Americans live and do not know how to solve. It's the plight of some of my classmates, who were fortunate enough to attend "excellent" suburban, public schools, yet still found a way to end up in jail.

On the other hand, the abolition of prisons seemed quite far-fetched to me. When it came to Colombia, in my opinion, the abolishment of prisons was not an option because of the delinquency that thrived there. Instead, Colombia needed to focus on inspiring people to work hard for their money, instead of planning schemes to get rich off of others' hard work. Also, the Colombian government needed to address the displacement of people and offer more social services to the poor so they did not have to rob or beg people for a living. The Colombian government needed to create an avenue where the poor could obtain an education and better jobs that earned more money than selling yogurt, gum and shoes on the streets.

In summary, it's important to be involved when you are living abroad so you have a better understanding of the culture. Volunteer with agencies that interest you. Go to events and listen to speakers who come to town. Watch the news. It will all help you better understand your new home.

Chapter 11:
Dance, Dance

Dance is a major part of Latino life, and much of it has to do with each nation's African influences. In the Dominican Republic, merengue and bachata were the genres of choice. Both styles of dance originated from the Dominican Republic. Children learned these dances from the time they could walk. As soon as you step off of the airplane, you'll hear this music everywhere you go.

Merengue is usually fast-paced and a two-step, kind of like a swaying of the hips back and forth to the beat. It's a partner dance and usually involves a lot of hip shaking and turns. To make the music, the bands use an accordion, a drum called the tambora, and a güira, which is similar to a maraca. Towards the 1990s, bands added a saxophone and bass guitar to the mix. The genre of music dates back to 1850, but it wasn't until Dictator Rafael Trujillo declared it the official music and dance of the country that it really became popular and started spreading to New York and Venezuela. Near Santiago, there's the prevalence of merengue típico, which is much faster and involves an accordion, and usually a band playing for the crowd. Some famous merengue artists are Juan Luis Guerra, Eddy Herrera, and Los Toros Band.

Whereas merengue was up tempo and fast-paced, bachata was more like the blues and singers often sang about relationships gone wrong. It's a slower and a more intimate dance, based off of a full eight-count moving within a square. The music is a mix of guitars, bongos, and the güira. It was created in the 1960s, but didn't really become popular until the 1980s and 90s. Early on, some popular singers were Luis Vargas and Antony Santos. But in the 2000s, the group Aventura, led by Anthony Romeo Santos, revolutionized the music and ended up selling out Madison Square Garden numerous times.

Both dances were easy to learn and were a lot of fun. In the Dominican Republic, this was what traditional clubs played. In the ritzy areas, they'd also play house and techno music. In the poorer areas, they'd mix this music with Spanish rap and reggaeton. But overall, merengue and bachata were the most popular genres of music in the Dominican Republic.

I'd frequently hear the music played at "rancho tipicos" with live bands. Dominican men had no problem asking a girl they never met to dance. Many times, they'd often try to dance really close, which I found to be a bit much if it was a man I just met. Some even tried to kiss me on the cheek while dancing. So, you'll definitely have to define your boundaries while dancing on the dance floor.

On the other hand, salsa was king in Colombia. The dance actually originated in New York City during the mid 20th century, with influences from Cuba and Puerto Rico, and American jazz. It evolved from Cuban dance forms including son, cha cha cha, and rumba. However, Colombians took the dance and created their own twist. Colombian salsa is known for quick, intricate footwork, along with lifts incorporated into the dancing. They add a lot of kicks and steps into their dancing.

Unlike other regions, most of the movement in Colombian salsa involves the hips and legs. Colombian salsa originated in Cali, and people there live for it. The city has deemed itself the World Capital of Salsa; there are tons of salsa schools there. Children there told me they had been dancing salsa since they were toddlers. That's all the nightclubs played. In all of the shops and restaurants, salsa was often the only music they played.

Colombians also danced salsa very differently from Puerto Ricans. They incorporated less turns and faster footwork. One downside was it was very difficult to find a dance partner in the club. Colombians go to the club as couples or in groups and they rarely mingle with people outside of their group. Your chances of meeting a dancing partner in the club are very slim. So, if you want to dance salsa, you'll have to bring your dance partner to the club with you.

While salsa was king in the city of Cali, in metropolises like Bogotá and Medellín, a lot of the upscale nightclubs would also mix reggaeton and techno into their rotations. Salsa may have been the king in Cali, but vallenato was the king on Colombia's northern, Caribbean coast. Vallenato is popular folk music in Colombia that is more like a slow dance. I had never heard of it until I moved there.

The music originated from Valledupar and was considered the music of the lower class and farmers as a way to spread messages. In the mid-1900s, it spread to every social group and is now a category in the Latin Grammy Awards. Every year, Valledupar hosts the Vallenato Legend Festival at the end of April. Some well-known vallenato performers are Guillermo Buitrago, Alejo Durán and Enrique Díaz. Grammy-Award winner Carlos Vives has helped the genre of music gain popularity around the world by combining it with pop music to create a new genre of music, vallenato pop.

Cumbia is to Barranquilla as vallenato is to Valledupar as salsa is to Cali. According to Discover Colombia, cumbia originates from the Magdalena River in Colombia. It's the perfect blend of the country's indigenous and African and European ancestry. The Africans infused the drums, giving it the musical rhythm, the indigenous brought the flute or gaita, making the music melodic, and the Europeans influenced the choreography and costume of its performers. The word cumbia comes from the African word cumbe which means dance. The music dates back to the late 1600s but didn't become very popular until 1950s and 1960s. Where in Colombia it originated is up for debate, but historians said it definitely came from an area near settlements of slaves. You'll find that cumbia is also widely accepted in Mexican culture, and often hear it in Mexican nightclubs.

Dancing to cumbia is similar to the salsa beat, but it involves more turning, almost as if someone is spinning in a wheel. It's an easier dance to learn than salsa, but slightly more difficult than merengue and bachata.

Reggaeton is very popular in Puerto Rico, Colombia, and Cuba. Back in 2010, it wasn't as popular in the Dominican Republic unless you were hanging out in the barrios of Santo Domingo. To me, it's similar to Hip Hop, except it's in Spanish with a chorus that usually sounds like a song and then a faster rap in between, all to an island reggae beat.

Reggaeton originated in Puerto Rico in the late 1990s, as underground music about drugs, violence, poverty, love and sex. "Dem Bow" was a popular song and early creators included DJ Playero, Ivy Queen, Don Chezina, and Baby Rasta y Gringo. The music genre became popular in the 2000s, known by the Dem Bow beat.

Reggaeton was one of my first loves. I came to know it in 2000, thanks to my cousin dating a Puerto Rican. It was this foreign music in Spanish that I loved dancing to. I began to sing along to Baby Rasta's "Cierra los Ojos Bien", not knowing what every word meant. That was my official introduction to Latin culture. However, reggaeton didn't really become popular in the United States until Tego Calderón, and Daddy Yankee started producing hits, along with Héctor & Tito, Nicky Jam, Luny Tunes, Zion & Lennox, and Don Omar during the mid-2000s. I remember my prom date bought me Daddy's Yankee's album when I was 16. Before then, I could never find a reggaeton CD in the store and would have to get them bootleg from my cousin.

During my time in the Dominican Republic, even though reggaeton still wasn't very popular there, Don Omar infused enough bachata into his music to make the Dominicans love him. I took a bus across the country to go to his concert in Santo Domingo. It was awesome. Two years later, Don Omar was performing in Colombia for carnival; of course I was there, too. He was even more popular then, as he performed in front of a huge crowd outdoors. Fast forward to 2016, Don Omar was in concert with Daddy Yankee in Orlando for the "Kings of Reggaeton" concert. I was there, too, and it was a blast hearing all of the songs from the past.

Reggaeton is now played on the radio stations in Florida as often as hip hop. I was pleased to find out Colombia had its own reggaeton stars from J Balvin, who recently crossed over into American airwaves and is singing hits with Pharrell, to Jiggy Drama to Maluma. In 2017, Beyoncé joined his hit, "Mi Gente". Puerto Rican reggaeton duo Plan B was also very popular in Colombia. Reggaeton was heard in a lot of the modern clubs in Colombia along with techno house beats. It was very popular in Medellín, where J Balvin is from. Most people grind to reggaeton music or what they call perreo. It involves one partner looking at the back of another, usually the woman grinding on the man.

Music and dance are a huge part of Latin culture. Some of my best memories have been on the dance floor. There's nothing like it. I suggest learning the popular music and dances of whichever country you plan to move to or visit beforehand and take lessons if you need to before you go. Going out dancing with friends is a popular social activity and you don't want to be left babysitting the wall. Also, take chances. Dance with different people. I had to stumble on the dance floor for an entire summer before I got the hang of the salsa beat.

Chapter 12:
Dating

Latin America is full of papis chulos or good-looking men. That's what a lot of women go there looking for. However, don't fall head over heels ladies. Looks aren't everything and if you don't slow your roll, you could end up enduring a lot of heartbreak, or face some serious consequences for falling in love so easily. This chapter is clearly about dating and I'll try my best to share the lessons I learned.

Lesson number 1: Beware of the married men. When I lived in the Dominican Republic, I was 19. I didn't even think to ask the guy I was seeing if he was married because in the United States, most people didn't get married at 19. I was naïve enough to think that if he was dating me, he must not be married to someone else. I met a guy named Juan* who I considered to be very attractive. We met in one of the beach towns at one of the nightclubs. We took late-night walks on the beach and he was very romantic.

He told me he was a baseball player and he'd be going to the states soon. I didn't know what to believe because he sure looked like one. When I came to visit him a few weeks after I met him, he informed me that he was headed to Santo Domingo for baseball and then headed to Kansas City. Being 19, I believed what he said, even though I was somewhat skeptical.

So I didn't return to that beach town after that because it reminded me too much of Juan, a man I had grown to be infatuated with. I didn't want to hang out in that town without him. Then, my friends begged me to go there for Semana Santa.

Lo and behold, when I got to the beach, there was Juan walking about. I yelled at him, "Hey I thought you were in the United States."

He said, "Oh, I hurt my shoulder and I got back today."

I knew then something was up, but I didn't press him more. We drank (it's legal to drink at 18 in the Dominican Republic) and danced and enjoyed ourselves. I just wanted to spend time with him. But he was still withholding the truth from me.

We hung out several more times. He lived on a compound with his family and we all had a barbecue. All of his family, except his mother, was very kind to me. They told me that I should date him and that he was a good guy. But while I was there, Juan stepped away a few times, telling me he had to speak to his "jefe". I assumed it was his baseball coach.

When I saw him again, at the end of my time in the Dominican Republic, we hung out at the beach and I cried at the end. That was the very last time I saw him. I called and talked to him once on the phone while I was in the United States. He told me he was getting ready to move to the United States for baseball. When I called back a month later, his family said he was in the United States. This was before WhatsApp and Facebook were popular.

I returned to the Dominican Republic the following year, in 2009, to complete a research project, but I also yearned to see Juan one more time. I called his home on my way to his family compound and that's when his uncle told me he wasn't there and, in fact, was living in New York City with his wife. My heart sank.

His uncle told me Juan never played baseball. He said Juan moved to the United States that previous year to be with his wife and that they got married in December 2007, a month before we'd met. At the time I met Juan, his uncle said he was waiting to get his visa papers together to move to the states, which is probably why he had to go to the capital so often. I realized that all of those times when his "jefe" was calling, it was probably her.

I asked his uncle why his mother was never very friendly toward me. He said, "Oh his wife bought her too." He told me that Juan never had to work, because his wife would send him money every week or two. She bought furniture for his mother's house and would visit every so often. After three years of it, he decided he might as well marry her. And that's how it happened.

I share this story to save you some heartache. Many of the island men are married or have women in the States. If you're going to get serious with them, make sure it's not a long-distance relationship but someone you can see every day, so you can evaluate if what they're telling you is the truth.

Even when you meet with men, try to determine whether they're being truthful. I had an instance where I interviewed a guy for my documentary and he invited me to the town bar. We were sitting there having a drink, along with everyone else in town, listening to merengue music, enjoying the breeze. He told me he had two kids and was divorced and that he had left his woman. I found out in about 20 minutes that he was lying. We were sitting there, talking, and having a decent time. Next thing I knew, this woman walked up from the side, out of his view and she slapped the hell out of his bald head right in front of me, and everyone else. She then dragged him by the ear out of the bar. Everyone in the area heard that slap. It was like the music stopped. I'm glad she didn't try to hurt me because it would've been an even bigger problem; it was so embarrassing. It was such a small town; I knew everyone was looking and knew he was out with the American. I just got up and walked away and returned to my hotel room.

So again, be careful of who you meet up with. I was there by myself filming so it wasn't like I had a group of girls to go out with. I enjoyed talking to the natives because that's how I learned about the community. It's also better to go places in groups, but when you're living there, that's not always an option.

Also, be aware of the sanky pankies—a Dominican word for men who prey on women from the United States, Canada, and Europe, hoping to make them fall in love with them so they can get a green card and escape the island. Most of the time, the desired foreigner is white. It's said that the man just wants the green card and pretends to love the woman, but once he's stateside, he leaves her and stays in the United States or Europe. Basically, they're looking for a sugar mama. There's even a movie about them, titled "Sanky Panky". Of course, not all Dominican men are playing this game, but it is popular.

There are plenty of Dominican women who do the same thing. Many of these sanky pankies work in the resorts, where they have easy access to tourists. As a traveler, you must remember many of these people have a slim chance of ever leaving the island. In order to get a tourist visa, you usually have to be wealthy, own property or a business, or the easiest option, get a fiancé visa by marrying someone from abroad. The system gives an incentive to these men to become sanky pankies if they believe leaving the island is their best chance at having a better life.

For women, it's tough because you may meet a man and both of you fall in love for the right reasons. Several of my friends abroad with me ended up getting married to Dominicans they met while abroad. You just have to make sure it's real love, and you're not being used for a visa. I've witnessed that, too. For me, it seemed easy to spot.

One weekend, I was at a resort in Punta Cana eating breakfast by myself. My server was a brown-skinned man. He didn't pay me much attention because I hadn't opened my mouth and he had no idea I wasn't Dominican.

Then, when I told him I was from the states, he said, "Oh, I love you."

I laughed and told him, "You don't love me. You just want to go to the United States." He asked for my number and I told him there was no reason to give him my number because I was returning to the United States soon.

He said, "Oh, I'll call you over there."

And I said, "No."

I didn't even know him. And didn't want to. But that's a sanky panky for you. Thirsty.

They didn't use the term sanky panky in Colombia, but they sure did have some gold diggers. One of my friends had a horrible experience. I share her story with you to make you aware, and less naïve when traveling abroad. I wouldn't want this painful experience to happen to another woman.

She was American. She decided to date a Colombian guy who looked Dominican or African American even. Now, I am not saying most Colombian men are like this or that even most black Colombian men are like this man, but I do believe that coming from poverty, without a college education, her boyfriend saw an American woman and he immediately saw dollar signs and an escape. He thought if he could put enough Rico Suave on her, he would get something out of it, whether it was a green card or a sugar mama.

So of course, she, like the rest of us, was young, and looking for love. He worked nights and had a low-paying job. He seemed nice. He was handsome and muscular. I didn't think anything of it.

Eventually, he caused a lot of drama in her life. He couldn't get off most nights to go out with us. He lived with his mother. His idea of fine dining was taking her out to eat at McDonald's. We used to take trips around the country and he could never afford to go. He couldn't do much of anything that involved money. By the way, these were issues I often encountered dating men in Latin America. As an American, you head over there with money to travel and explore, but finding a male companion to travel with, especially if your companion isn't white, will be difficult because many of them do not have the money to live that lifestyle. And the ones that do are usually already in a relationship.

So, he couldn't go on trips or do anything that involved money, but he convinced my friend to make big purchases. He encouraged her to buy a moto, knowing it was way too crowded on the Bogotá streets for her to be driving it anywhere. She bought it and he drove it most of the time.

One winter night, we were all in a taxi riding home from the club and she mentioned she was missing hundreds of dollars. She said she kept it in her dresser drawer. She suspected either the cleaning lady or her landlord took it. Her landlord told her he didn't take it and the cleaning lady denied taking it also. We all told her it was probably her man who stole her money, but she didn't want to believe us. She said she had left him alone once in her room to take a shower. We tried to tell her that it had to have been him that stole her money, and she should stop seeing him.

I guess she asked him if he stole her money and she said he looked her in the eyes and said he'd never do that. She believed him at the time and continued dating him. This was the same friend whose boyfriend protected her from the gay teen who broke into her apartment, demanding he be paid for the sex. From then on, I believe she saw him as her protector in this foreign place, which made it harder for her to leave him.

If he was going to be her protector, she had to be his provider, whether she agreed to it or not. So she lent him money, hundreds of dollars. She paid for their meals and a lot of other things. Heck, unlike me, she had recently come into some money so it didn't seem to faze her much.

She was not watching her money and he knew it. Even when her boyfriend stole from her the first time, she was unsure exactly how much was taken because she never kept track of how much she threw in the drawer. The money she gave him wasn't enough for him, though. She learned days before leaving Colombia for good that he had been stealing from her during their entire ten-month relationship. Robbing her blind; he left her broke.

When she showered, when she went to sleep, when he'd hold her wallet, he was stealing her cash. He told her he even knew her pin to her American bank account and was taking her bank card to the ATM to get cash out when she wasn't looking. She was paying for everything and had lent him money. He still felt the need to rob her of more than $2,000, she said.

She told me all of this and said it left her with a sour taste in her mouth. She didn't want to date a Colombian ever again. But not everyone had this experience; it didn't happen to me. These are the things to be cautious of when you're a foreigner, especially a woman, living in Colombia.

In my experience, I found dating to be extremely difficult in Colombia because it's not their custom to talk to strangers in public. The culture is very cliquish. So in order to meet a guy, you'd have to be introduced by someone. What I did was go on my Colombian friends' Facebook pages and browse through all of their friends. If I found someone attractive, I friend requested them. That's how I met the guy I dated most of my time in Colombia. He was Afro-Colombian, from the Pacific coast and a police officer. Two months into our relationship, the government sent him away to Valledupar. We were only able to see each other a few times after that. It was only when I could afford to fly there and visit. However, we talked and Skyped on the phone every night and became very close. I found dating to be rewarding because it allowed me to really learn about Colombian culture and its intricacies. For instance, on our first date, he asked the waiter for plastic gloves so he could eat his fried chicken. I asked what the gloves were for and he said so his hands didn't get greased up. I told him that eating chicken was supposed to be messy and that in the United States, we didn't do that. He joked that Colombia was a more advanced country. We both got a chuckle out of that and that's when I figured I had met my match.

Unfortunately, the ways of society got to us and our cultural differences were too large to ignore. I met his family in Quibdó and spent a weekend with them. They were very friendly and we got along well. I was sitting in a room with his brother and he was showing me pictures. Then, he stumbled upon a picture of a little boy in the lap of his brother, the guy I was dating. The boy was light skinned but looked just like him. I asked who the kid was and he confirmed it was his brother's. He had never mentioned to me he had a son, three months into our relationship. The son lived in Medellín with his mother. Again, young and naïve, he said I never asked him so he didn't feel the need to tell me. That was discouraging. Then, I started to realize that he had difficulties managing his money. He lived for the day and didn't plan for tomorrow. Also, he kept saying he didn't believe a life in the United States would be any better for him than his life in Colombia. As my time in Colombia came to a close, I started to realize that the fairytale of bringing him back to the United States with me and making it work, even though he barely spoke English and hadn't finished college, was going to make my life very difficult, when it didn't have to be.

I had planned on seeing him again before I left Colombia, but I had to leave a few weeks early due to my grandmother having terminal cancer and coming to her end. I broke the news that I was returning to the United States and wouldn't be able to see him before left. I remember him asking *for good*, and I said *yes*. It was a very sad phone call. I was crying the entire day as I packed my things in a haste, sad I didn't get to say goodbye in person to a lot of people.

After I left, the Skype calls between he and I stopped, but we did message each other every now and then on Facebook. We had a long conversation around the New Year of 2014 and had planned to meet up later that year. I was at a point in my life where I wanted to be in a serious relationship but wasn't having any luck and I began to wonder what life would be like had we stayed together.

Around the same time, I met my husband and our relationship got serious fast. I broke that news to him in April, when he randomly asked me on Facebook one day if I was still coming to Colombia. He was happy for me. A month later, I learned from his sister he died suddenly from a heart attack. He was 33 years old. I couldn't believe it. At one point in my life, we were close and it hurt to know his life got cut so short.

I share with you this story to encourage you to date while living abroad. It will enrich your experience and create some of your best memories. However, be smart and keep your eyes open. Don't let them take advantage of you. Hang out with them at night in groups, with your friends. That way your friends make sure you get home safely. Ask questions. And remember, their actions speak louder than their words. No matter how much they tell you "I love you", pay attention to what they do. It lets you know if they actually take you seriously, or if you're just a fling or experiment. That way you don't get your heart broken, or scammed out of a lot of money.

Stephanie Claytor

Chapter 13:
Checkpoints

Along with having members of the Colombian army stationed everywhere, the National Police had what they called puestos de control. They randomly set up cones in the middle of any street or on any pedestrian bridge, usually near the TransMilenio stops in urban areas. Then, they *randomly* selected any car, bus, or pedestrian to check. They asked for your cédula or identification card and in the case of men, they patted them down searching for weapons and looked inside of their bags.

This random selection did not seem random to me. From my observations, almost all of the teenage boys who were selected for searches appeared to be poor. This may have been because in Colombia, it was mandatory for men to register for the draft at 18. It's my understanding that those who were exempt from the draft had a libreta militar. Exemptions were given to college students, heads of households, the displaced, and those who paid to avoid the draft. The police were checking for these cards and if a young man was stopped at the puestos de control and didn't have his libreta militar, he was put into a truck and taken away to serve. I later learned what I was witnessing was called a batida or round up.

During these random checks, the police reportedly looked at the cedulas and radioed the nearest station to check if the person had violated any laws or had any warrants for their arrest.

I was stopped once while trying to enter the TransMilenio station. The police officer asked for my cedula and when he saw I had a foreigner's cedula and was not Colombian, he let me go. So it's very important to have your foreigner identification card or a copy of your passport, in case you come across one of these puestos de control. In the Dominican Republic, too. They had puestos de control, but they mainly were checking for Haitians near the border.

In Colombia, it appeared to me that people who dressed or looked outside of the norm, such as people who didn't wear business attire and instead wore baggy pants, or Gothic attire, or who had an afro or dreadlocks, were more prone to be searched.

What mystified me was the fact that they could select anyone from a crowd, pat them down, and look through their belongings without reasonable suspicion they did anything wrong. In the TransMilenio, this happened often. They selected young boys from the crowds and especially homeless people, put them against the wall, and patted them down. It looked like a segment out of the television show "Cops" when they patted folks down during traffic stops as they prepared to arrest them. And again, this was normal behavior.

Bogotá was militarized back then. In fact, in the neighborhood across the highway from my apartment, where the wealthy lived, there were armed security guards watching apartment buildings. Most of the TransMilenio stations and bridges had a police officer or soldier guarding them. Most of the stores had several armed guards. Coming from a small town in Ohio, I never saw a soldier in uniform until I got to Syracuse, and that was only because Fort Drum was nearby. Seeing armed guards was a new reality for me while I lived there, but it slowly became my new normal.

So again, in order to keep yourself safe and out of trouble, if one of the guards stops you, show them your identification and don't make a scene. Remember you're in their country and therefore have to follow their laws. Have your foreigner's identification card with you. Hopefully they will let you go and not try to pat you down or search your things.

Chapter 14:
Healthcare

A good resource to check out before moving abroad is the United States' Centers for Disease Control and Prevention website. It reminds travelers to be up-to-date on all routine vaccinations, such as measles-mumps-rubella (MMR), tetanus vaccine, chickenpox vaccine, and polio vaccine. For Colombia, it recommends travelers get a Hepatitis A vaccine, along with a Typhoid vaccine. Both diseases can be contracted by eating contaminated food or water. If you're planning on being sexually active, or getting a tattoo or piercing, the CDC recommends getting a Hepatitis B vaccine. If you'll be spending a lot of time outdoors, a Rabies vaccine is suggested, along with taking malaria medicine. The CDC suggests travelers to the Dominican Republic take the same precautions.

Colombia and the Dominican Republic are also dealing with the spread of the Zika virus, which is primarily spread by mosquitoes. According to the CDC, Zika usually doesn't live at elevations above 6,500 feet, so people traveling to cities such as Bogotá and Medellín are at minimal risk of contracting Zika from a mosquito. However, travelers to these destinations are still at risk of contracting the disease through sexual intercourse. CDC recommends using condoms, avoiding sharing sexual toys, or refraining from having sex in order to prevent the sexual transmission of Zika.

Colombians, especially Bogotános, always attempted to be formal and polite. Ever since the H1N1 scare, they took up the custom of wearing surgical masks around their mouth and nose when they had any type of cold or cough. Because we, people living in Colombia, were often in crowded areas, such as public transportation, I actually liked this custom and joined the Bogotános when they directed mean stares toward people who coughed up a storm and forgot to wear their mask. As a matter of fact, this was so pronounced that one elderly man in his 60s held up the line to board the airplane because the woman in front of him was coughing, without covering her mouth or wearing a mask. The woman, wearing leggings, fur snow boots, a scarf, and a tank top in 45-degree weather, who apparently was returning from Belgium, had the nerve to say she was cold and didn't know why she kept coughing.

That's just one example of Colombians dealing with illness. When I was teaching in Colombia, my program provided me with health insurance. I had to go to the clinic once. It seemed to be a normal process. My appointment wasn't set up in advance. I had some stomach pains and a student walked with me to the clinic next to the college. I told the receptionist my stomach hurt. I waited a few minutes, met with the doctor, attempted to explain what was wrong in Spanish, and she gave me a prescription. I went to the local drug store near my home and filled the prescription. I got better in a few days.

It was quite the contrary in the Dominican Republic. During my first days there, my class group went on a field trip to the public hospital. It was awful! It reeked in there. I went to the bathroom only to find out there wasn't any toilet paper or soap. I then wondered what type of care they would provide if they couldn't afford to have toilet paper and soap in the bathroom. That's when I decided I wouldn't do anything that would necessitate me going to the hospital. That was my worst fear living there. However, I was told that the private hospitals were very nice, but expensive.

Another thing I found peculiar in Colombia was birth control. When I visited the pharmacy, I only saw the Yaz birth control pill being sold over the counter but I read many other pills were available. The pharmacist offered to give me a shot of birth control. He said all I had to do was go in the back room and bend over and he could administer the shot in my behind. I looked at him like he was crazy, but apparently that was the norm. To me, it seemed easier to bring your own birth control rather than trying what they had to offer. It's available in Colombia, but it may not be the brand you prefer. Also, they sell menstrual pads in the drugstores but have a smaller variety of tampons, and they usually sell them without applicators. The most popular brand is Nosotras. Condoms, however, were prevalent there, but they did not have Magnum sizes. Just regular latex condoms and not a large variety. To get tested for a sexually transmitted disease, many visited Pro Familia clinics, which was similar to Planned Parenthood in the States.

One thing about Bogotá that I appreciated was home delivery. You could get practically anything delivered to your house. Places like drug stores, supermarkets, and liquor stores all delivered whatever you wanted to buy right to your doorstep. And this was for no extra charge. I never imagined how much this would come in handy.

Overall, I'd say don't be too concerned with getting sick. Get the recommended shots before you go. Avoid eating food sold on the street because you don't know how it was prepared. Don't drink the tap water and make sure restaurants are providing you with bottled water. Bring your medications and prescriptions with you, along with enough supply to last the entire time you're there. And of course, wear insect repellant and sunscreen.

Stephanie Claytor

Chapter 15:
The Weather

Colombia experienced a horrible rain season (May to November) while I was there. There was more rainfall than many people said they had seen in their lifetime; it affected everyone. In my case, the water leaked into my bedroom, causing me to be stressed out during the beginning of my stay because the repairman couldn't figure out how to resolve the problem. I also had to speak to him in Spanish about plumbing. However, I had it good. Thousands of other Colombians experienced more serious problems, such as losing their homes. According to the BBC, two million people were affected by the floods and landslides during the latter part of 2010, which led to three hundred people dying. After visiting Cartagena one weekend, I passed by one village, where every home was at least halfway under water. It reminded me of images of Katrina. The town was for the most part deserted.

Other than the rain, the weather was mild the rest of the year. The temperature in each city remained steady, due to the country's close proximity to the equator. The cities in the mountains, Medellín, and Bogotá, were cooler. The higher in elevation, the cooler it was. Bogotá had a temperature that ranged between 50- and 60-degrees Fahrenheit throughout the year. It always seemed to rain around 4PM. After the sun would go down, you definitely needed a jacket. Often, it was cloudy, but on some occasions the sun would come out.

Medellín was warmer—similar to California weather, with temperatures ranging in the 60s and 70s. There wasn't a lot of humidity. Cali was the same way, with more sunshine and the temperatures were in the 70s and 80s. Then there were the Atlantic and Pacific coasts, where it got hot and humid and the temperature hovered in the high 80s.

When it came to severe weather, the main things to worry about were floods, landslides, avalanches, and on rare occasions, hurricanes on the Atlantic coast, mainly in the northeast corner of the country.

My advice would be to bring leather jackets and boots if you're moving to Bogotá. Buy a comforter because the homes don't have heat, and make sure the house has a good supply of hot water. If you're living on the coasts, you won't need a lot of jeans. It is really hot there. Basically, check the average temperatures of where you're moving to because in Colombia, it varies greatly.

In the Dominican Republic, however, it was hot year-round. The climate is similar to Florida's—a cold night would be in the 60s. In the wintertime, the temperatures hovered around the 70s and 60s at night. You'll want to bring a leather jacket for those nights and a few cardigans because they love to blast the air conditioner inside of buildings. The main thing you'll have to worry about are hurricanes. Hurricane season begins in June and lasts through November. That is also the rainy season, so prepare for daily downpours if you're there during that time. In the spring, when I was there, the weather was lovely and it hardly ever rained.

Chapter 16:
Religion

Even though I grew up as a United Methodist attending church every Sunday, the days of going to church faithfully were long gone for me before I set sail abroad. I guess I was disheartened my first year of college when I couldn't find a church I identified with, so I stopped going altogether.

So, when I arrived in Colombia, upon graduation, church wasn't the first thing that came to mind. Honestly, attending church didn't seem to be much of a priority within Colombia either. It wasn't like living in the southern part of the United States, which I would later learn, where one of the first questions people asked you when they met you was what church you attended. As a matter of fact, I don't recall that question ever coming up in Colombia.

There were churches, but I don't recall them being on every corner as in the States. Many of the cities did have historic cathedrals that were usually in the center of town, but religion in Colombia was much different from what I assumed—that everyone would be Catholic.

I would always see these long lines in my neighborhood on Sundays, outside a building close to my house; the lines that wrapped around the block. It piqued my curiosity and, one day, I decided to visit the church. On this Sunday, about 1,000 people filled the auditorium.

What struck me during the service was their method of praise. All of a sudden, the stage lit up with bright, colorful strobe lights. Then a band came on stage and the congregation stood up. Suddenly, the place turned into a rock concert. The people started jumping up and down yelling, "Grita por Jesus" or "Scream for Jesus!" I soon realized this was a contemporary, non-denomination service, similar to the larger congregations in the U.S. The only difference was everything was in Spanish. The service was quick and the pastor wore a purple, button-up shirt and jeans. He said he didn't wear a corbata or tie because he wanted to keep the younger people coming to his church. Apparently, it was working because there were plenty there.

The service was another one of those moments that made me realize how alike we were, Americans and Colombians, as human beings. Although that style of service wasn't ideal for me, I knew that many churches functioned similarly in the United States.

According to the United States State Department International Religious Freedom Report for 2012, there are varying numbers for how many Colombians identify with being Catholic. The numbers range from 90 percent, according to the Roman Catholic Bishops Conference, to 80 percent from news sources. I can tell you from my experience living in Bogotá, religion rarely came up as a topic of conversation. Of course, identifying with and practicing a religion are two different things.

Estimates indicate Protestants make up 14 percent of the population of 47 million, according to the Colombian Evangelical Council and around five percent of the population belonged to other faiths, including Muslims and Jews. Another five percent of the population identified with atheism. Many of the people who blended Catholicism with African animism were typically Afro-Colombians living on the Pacific coast. Many of the Jews lived in major cities, and many of the Muslims lived on the Caribbean coast.

In 1991, there were several, constitutional reforms that led to removing the Roman Catholic Church as the state church, and the protection of religious freedom. Discrimination on basis of religion was prohibited. According to the report, the constitution also recognized the right of parents to choose the type of education their children receive, including religious instruction and that no student shall be forced to receive religious education in public schools. Similar to practices in the United States, a Constitutional Court ruling obligated schools to have alternative accommodations for students based on their religion, following the petition of a Seventh-day Adventist University student who requested to miss class on Saturday.

While the Colombians practiced a separation of church and state, Good Friday, Christmas and many other Catholic holidays are still national holidays. On the other hand, Roman Catholicism was still the official religion of the Dominican Republic, even though the constitution provided for freedom of religion and belief.

Catholicism being the official religion in the country was very obvious upon arrival. It was one of the first things I learned about my host family upon moving in; they were devout Catholics. My host mom had a painting of Jesus in her home and bibles and crosses in several rooms. She always attended Mass, and talked about the work of God daily.

Also, every time I left the house, she said, "Qué te vaya bien, y con

82

Dios," meaning, "I hope that everything goes well on your journey, and that you go with God by your side." She and many other Dominicans would often say, "Si Dios quiere," or "God-willing" about everything. That included making it to appointments on time, and even making it home safely, or waking up the next day, or planning anything in the future.

The U.S. government estimated 10.5 million people live in the Dominican Republic, as of July 2015. According to a 2014 Pew Research study, 57 percent of them were Catholic, 23 percent were Protestant, including Pentecostals, and Mennonites, and 18 percent didn't have a religious affiliation.

The 2015 United States State Department Report on International Religious Freedom reported the nation had around 350 Jews, who primarily lived in the nation's capital, and around 3,000 Muslims, who were mostly college students. The report also indicated that most of the Haitian immigrants were Catholic and it was unknown how many practiced Voodoo or other African Caribbean beliefs, such as Santeria.

According to the report, the Dominican government extended special privileges to the Catholic Church. For instance, the Catholic Church had the authority to revise all textbooks used in public schools throughout the country, according to its concordat. Likewise, while not always enforced, the law required bible studies in all public schools. Private schools were exempt from the practice and the law allowed for parents to excuse their children from religious studies in public schools.

When I taught in the public school, I didn't witness bible study classes. Honestly, with the teachers calling in sick and the immense challenges they were dealing with in terms of poverty, their main concern was making sure the children could read and write in Spanish, and also teaching the children some English.

When it comes to religion, I believe in either country, you can find a place to worship if that is your desire. Walk around the main downtowns and visit churches. My experience was they welcomed me with open arms. If your host family is more religious than you are, participate in their ceremonies and respect them. Don't be judgmental. You're there to learn.

Stephanie Claytor

Chapter 17:
The Help

While hanging out in Cartagena, one dinner date with my American friends has always stuck with me. It was the day before New Year's Eve and we were eating at this nice Italian restaurant in Boca Grande. While discussing the day's issues at the table, this Beamer SUV pulled up to the curb and out walks this family, mostly white and mestizo. That was rarer on the Caribbean coast. Then, there was a brown-skinned, black woman with them. She was wearing nurse scrubs while they were all dressed up for dining. They came and ate near us while she proceeded to take the baby and go sit in the other room. It was then that I realized she was the nanny. While they sipped on wine and talked, she sat in the other room, holding the baby. She appeared to be in her late 30s or 40s.

It reminded me of my own great grandmother who was a maid back in the 1930s and 40s and I realized this was what she must have gone through. To me, it felt strange. I thought this was 2011. I'd heard of people hiring nannies in the States to babysit their children. But, bringing them out to dinner, too? And the uniform, differentiating her from the family and identifying her as the maid, it just seemed extra and demeaning. Apparently this was the practice for the rich in Colombia, so don't be surprised if you see it. That was my only experience seeing the nanny in Colombia, but I didn't hang with the rich and famous.

I'll admit we did have a maid come once a month. They're called "ama de casa" or "empleada de la casa." We were living in a four-bedroom apartment with white tile. My roommate was hardly there. With the white tile and constant rain, every time you walked on it, there were footprints everywhere. I found myself mopping tile constantly in my spare time. And I didn't have time for that. I was there to have fun, not clean house. So about three months in, I told my roommate I was ready to pay for help.

She said we could call "Martha." Now, growing up, I was taught you should clean your own house. And I was skeptical of having strangers in my home who could have access to my things, especially my American passport (worth gold in my opinion and probably one of the most important things I owned).

So, I said Martha could come, once a month on my days off. I didn't want her in my room or washing my clothes. We contracted her to clean the kitchen, bathrooms, and mop the hallway, kitchen, and living rooms floors. It was a godsend. Martha could clean the silver in the kitchen better than I ever could. She also did a great job cleaning the floors. We paid her minimum wage, the equivalent of $30 for about four hours of work, once a month. Even though I felt some type of way about having a maid, it really did help me enjoy my experience more. My roommate had hired Martha before. She appeared to be indigenous and didn't talk much. She just came over, cleaned and left. When I departed Colombia in a hurry, I had a ton of stuff that I could not take back with me to the States. Martha and I were the same size. So, I left her shoes, blankets, and clothes. I don't know if she used them, but I hope so because they were nice things.

If you're headed to Colombia and want a maid, I'd just suggest asking neighbors or friends. They can probably give you a good recommendation. There's also a new site called Hogaru.com that is helpful, if you're living in Bogotá, Medellín, or Cali.

According to an article written by Elyssa Pachico in the Huffington Post, Colombian law requires domestic servants to be paid Colombia's minimum monthly wage, which is about $333. Their employers are also required to pay for their benefits. According to the National Union School study, about 62 percent of those surveyed said they earned less than the minimum wage, even though the majority worked over the legal limit of 10 hours per day.

Colombia has SINTRASEDON, a national union for domestic workers. It's been active for more than 30 years. The union is based in Medellín and focuses on lobbying for Afro-Colombian domestic workers, although it is open to workers from all backgrounds. Afro-Colombians make up the majority of Medellín's domestic labor force, according to the article.

Also, one of my Colombian friends said she learned her English by becoming an au pair in New York. She signed up for the program and lived with a rich family, caring for their kids while they worked. She lived with them for at least a year and became part of the family. She said the experience helped improve her English immensely. I met her upon her return to Colombia. Apparently, being an au pair is one avenue for Colombian women to get a visa to the United States, to work as nannies. Looking online, it appears these women work as au pairs for as low as $100 to $200 a week, but of course you're paying for their lodging and food.

I didn't notice it as much in Colombia, but in the Dominican

Republic, the apartments and houses were built with separate quarters for the maids and nannies. For instance, in our apartment, there was a really small room that was for the maid. It was big enough for a bed. They also had their own bathroom near the laundry. In many of the homes, they hired maids to clean them, usually poor women from rural areas who needed a job. In my home, we didn't have a maid because my host family couldn't afford it and didn't need it since my host mom wasn't working.

Although it may seem strange for an American, especially a black American, if you find yourself cleaning all of the time and not enjoying yourself, don't feel ashamed to ask for help. When searching for a host family or roommate, find out if they have someone helping to clean the house, so you're aware. Just always know where your passport and stash of cash are hidden because you don't want them to come up missing.

Chapter 18:
Beauty

Beauty in Latin America—that's a topic I could go on about for days. It is of utmost importance, at all times, I can tell you that. I remember being in the Dominican Republic and getting stares for wearing leggings and a long, loose shirt while walking down the street. And don't even venture to wear pajama pants outside in Santiago. That was a no-no. Women in Santiago dressed up and put on talcones or high-heeled shoes even when they went to the grocery store. I recall a lot of the clothes being fitted in the Dominican Republic. Lots of tight jeans and shirts and sandals.

In the Dominican Republic, to be beautiful meant to have tan skin and long, straight hair. In fact, women were considered rebels if they didn't straighten their hair. Straight hair was a symbol of professionalism. Dominican women were fascinated with "pelo malo" (bad hair) and "pelo bueno" (good hair). Unfortunately, if you ask a Dominican what pelo malo is, they will usually associate it with hair that has more African kinky features, and if you ask them what pelo bueno is, it's almost always associated with straight hair and more European characteristics.

Also, having natural blonde hair and blue eyes was admired by many there because practically no one had it naturally but foreigners. They treated it like royalty. It was a part of the culture for women to long for their, "principe azul" or prince charming with blue eyes.

I remember in the home where I lived, if I went to the beach and came back with my curly hair, my host mom would encourage me to go to the salon so I could have pelo bueno. The hair salon was the factory for blanqueamiento, or whitening of the race. The women there couldn't necessarily control their skin color, but they could control the texture of their hair. The salon was where women would dye their hair blonde or withstood whatever it took to get their hair straight so they would come off as more Spanish and indigenous, and less black, which they equated to being Haitian.

There were hair salons on every corner. Most women got their hair done often. They'd usually get the Dominican blow-out, where they'd wash their hair and blow it out with a blow dryer, or put big rollers in the hair and sit under the dryer. The blowers and the dryers were extremely hot, meant to get all of those kinks out. Dominican salons are famous for being able to take any hair texture and transform it to bone straight. However, I found that the hair may look straight in the salon, but as soon as the humidity hit it, it went back to being poofy again. Most of the Dominican salons I went to did not use hot water or flat irons, strangely enough. Also, getting your toes and nails painted was essential. Fortunately, the manicures, pedicures and getting your hair done cost way less than in the United States. I believe that's why it's so popular there.

The women always wore makeup in public. A lot of makeup was definitely the norm. In fact, my host mother told me when her husband was alive, she woke up before him and had her hair and makeup done before he got up. She said it was expected.

Of course, this was the standard in Santiago. While visiting the rural areas outside of Santo Domingo, it was a different story. The women wore night gowns around their neighborhood. They wore rollers in their hair all day with a scarf around the rollers to keep them in place, partially because they didn't have electricity half of the day so they had to let the hair air dry. It was a much more relaxed environment in the campo. Through these observations, I realized the straightening of hair and the manicures and pedicures were symbols of race and social class. People judged where you were from and your social class based on your hair, feet, and hygiene.

While there, I completed a project on what I considered to be Afro-Dominican women, asking them about their identity. I'll never forget one of my friend's host mother's responses. She had beautiful, brown skin and her hair had a little kink to it, but was straighter than most black people's. I asked her did she consider herself black. She said no and explained to me that she was "indio". She said her ancestors came from the indigenous Taíno and from Spain and her family didn't have a trace of African ancestry in it. I had read about Dominicans denying their black heritage but it was very memorable to sit and have a conversation with someone I knew and have them deny it straight to my face. The woman was almost as dark as chocolate. Nevertheless, it's a complex issue in the Dominican Republic and if you're a black tourist visiting there, it puts you in an awkward position.

Dominicans have a million names for skin colors, all to help them refrain from calling themselves black. Blanco is white. Mestizo is white mixed with Indian. Trigueño is a little bit more yellow, olive skin, with curly or straight hair. Indio was the term recognized nationwide, which to Dominicans meant somewhere in between black and white. Moreno is dark-skinned, closer to black. Negro or prieto is black, and when prieto was used, it was often in a derogatory manner in the Dominican Republic.

Dominicans also refer to each other by their skin color. When trying to get someone's attention, instead of calling them by their name, or if they do not know their name, they'll say something like "morena, ven aca," which translates to "Dark-skinned girl, come here."

Sometimes you'll hear family members use the word negro or negra in an endearing, caring type of manner and tell each other, "Ay mi negra, estas bella," which means "Aww mi black girl, you are beautiful."

In Colombia, beauty standards were slightly different. Makeup and straight hair was still the norm, although some black women donned braids and weaves. Beauty pageants were also a big deal in Colombia. Blonde hair and redheads were definitely very rare. Other than that, Colombians came in all shades, from black to white. The ideal Colombian woman was curvaceous and plastic surgery was popular. There were very few Asians.

According to the International Society of Aesthetic Plastic Surgery, Colombia came in eighth place for the most body enhancement procedures in 2014, with more than 357,000 procedures. It came behind the United States, Brazil, Japan, South Korea, Mexico, Germany, and France. Also, Colombia's cosmetic surgeries are drawing lots of tourists.

Medellín is known for its cosmetic surgery centers. I remember one of my colleagues who worked in a university in Medellín told me about her students bragging about their boob jobs as a gift from their parents for their eighteenth birthday. It was like a transition into adulthood. Plastic surgery centers were everywhere, from the malls to the hospitals.

If you're thinking of getting some work done, you'll want to make sure the doctor is licensed and the medical clinic is authorized by the government.

Colombians also cared very much about their skin. I don't recall seeing too many people walking around with acne. In fact, my face broke out while I was there and I remember hanging out with some Colombians at an apartment get-together.

The women literally pulled me aside and said, "¿Qué le pasó a tu cara?" or "What happened to your face?" I was shocked and embarrassed because an American would never ask that question because acne was normal, but these women were serious. I told them it's always been like that and I've tried everything. They got out pens and paper and wrote down products I needed to ask for at the pharmacy because in their minds, it was unacceptable for me to walk around with a breakout. Having tried everything, I actually listened to them and bought some hydroquinone, which is actually a skin lightener. I learned they sold it over there in a higher dosage than in the United States. They told me to rub it on my face at night and that it'd get all of the dirt out of my skin and lighten the brown bumps on my face. It did seem to work. My skin was clear when I left there, but that just goes to show how they feel about bad skin.

While living in Colombia, I discovered there was a magazine similar to Ebony called Ebano created by Esaud Urrutia Noel, an Afro-Colombian journalist from Cali. The purpose of the magazine was to highlight blacks who were succeeding. Noel said before his magazine was created, blacks were only represented in Colombian sports, or folklore. He wanted to show them in the fields of medicine, agriculture, and economic development. He wanted black Colombian children to know they could aspire to be more than just athletes or play secondary roles in soap operas.

Noel said eventually the magazine would discuss Colombia's identity crisis, which he referred to as endoracismo, or the racism or discrimination against one's own race. He said many Colombians didn't want to identify with being black if their skin was a light brown hue because they knew if they identified with being black, they assumed their opportunities would be fewer in Colombia. He called that a big issue on the Caribbean coast.

In Colombia, there was every skin shade. In the Andes region, the center of the country, people were generally paler, with more olive skin and black hair and a shorter stature. Then, on the Pacific coast, the majority of the people were dark-skinned, as if you had stepped into Ghana. There were also many indigenous living there. On the Caribbean coast, the people generally looked more Caribbean—somewhere in between black and white, with tan skin and varying hair textures. Even in the Caribbean, there were indigenous and historic black communities. Then, there was San Andrés, a Colombian island. Dreadlocks, braids, and brown skin was more popular there, which is a great segue into the next chapter.

Chapter 19:
Skin Tone Matters

In my opinion, people are treated differently in Latin America based on the color of their skin, the texture of their hair, and by the way they dress. You could probably say that about the United States as well, but I guess I expected it at home and it didn't feel as overt.

Let's begin with the incident that I will never forget. The U.S. Embassy paid for my friend and I to give talks about American Black History to predominantly Afro-Colombian schools during Black History Month. We did one presentation in Quibdó, Colombia, and another in Cali, Colombia, the city with one of the largest black populations in the country. After our first presentation in Cali, we returned to our hotel. It was one of the nicest and most expensive hotels in Cali. I was dressed in my cute, pink dress and donning my auburn fro, with black stilettos to cover my feet. My American friend who was with me, was dark-skinned, wearing a suit, and his hair was cut in a fade. We were dressed professionally, which really shouldn't even matter.

As we approached the door to the hotel, I noticed the security guard moved in front of it to block it and he then raised his gun over his body. He stood in front of us, blocking the doorway and asked us "Necesitan ayuda (You all need help)?" From his body language, I interpreted it as "Let me help you find out where you are going. You must be lost because you couldn't possibly be staying here."

I was upset because I realized right away what was going on. My friend responded in a polite manner because he didn't quite get it. "No, we're fine," he said.

I told the security guard, "No, no necessito ayuda. Me voy a mi habitación." I then proceeded to walk through the door. What made the situation even worse was that the security guard was the same color as me. I felt that he concluded that we didn't belong in that hotel simply because of the color of our skin. He was literally blocking the door with a gun raised. What else was I supposed to think? It appeared to me that this black security guard had internalized racism to the extent that he discriminated against his own people. It got worse.

At the same hotel, I was interviewing on camera the owner of Ebano magazine in the hotel's restaurant. When the magazine owner brought his fruit drink, the waiter said "tú" to him, instead of "usted".

The owner of the magazine caught the disrespect right away. He called the server over and said, "You are disrespecting me. You do not call me tú." Tú means 'you', but it is used with people one knows. The formal version is usted, used with adults and people one doesn't know as a sign of respect—Spanish 101. The waiter apologized and said he worked on a cruise ship and everyone had a different way of speaking Spanish and some, like the Argentines, don't take tú and usted that seriously. The magazine owner wasn't buying it.

He later said to me, "Well he's in Colombia now and he should know how to treat his customers with respect." The waiter was also a black man.

In the Dominican Republic, it was the same nonsense. It was so bad that when I went out, I had to think about who I was going out with because there would be limitations as to where they could go.

Many of the American black girls that were studying at the college with me had natural hairstyles, mostly afros. In the Dominican Republic, I had relaxed hair that I wore mostly straight. Most of the nicer clubs refused to let my friends in.

The club bouncers simply told them, "No you cannot come in' or "It's a private party." Hell, I even got told this when I straightened my hair and went with my Dominican friend. I was black and she was just as black as me but bigger, what they called gordita. We were trying to get into a ritzier club in Santiago.

The bouncers at the door looked us over and said, "It's a private party tonight."

We said, "OK", and hopped back into the cab. We just wanted to see if the rumors were true. One of my friends over there, had long beautiful natural hair. Instead of flat ironing it straight, she chose to blow dry it. So, it was half straight, half frizzy, and long as in down to her bra strap. She went to a club in downtown Santiago and she said the bouncers told her she had to put her hair in a ponytail in order to be admitted into the club. Crazy, right?

Another instance I'll never forget while living in Santiago was when I went with my same Dominican American friend, to a rancho tipico (a place where they play merengue music). We got our table near the dance floor and sat there for more than an hour. No one asked us to dance. Then, my brown-skinned American friend showed up with our classmates, who happened to be white with blonde hair. We all got a table in front of the dance floor. The men flew over there like ants, one after the other. And they went straight to the white girls and asked for their hands to dance. However, there was one problem—the white women didn't know how to dance, and felt embarrassed to dance merengue so they said *no*. Then, feeling embarrassed, the men asked around the table, starting from the lightest women to us, the black women.

As we traveled closer to the border with Haiti, more problems arose. The group I was studying with always took weekend vacations. We would travel around the country in a van. Well, most of my classmates were white and only one of my classmates was brown skinned, but she straightened her hair. She was what they considered morena. Of course, us black folks somehow always chose to sit in the back of the van. So, when we traveled near the border, the security checkpoints started popping up along the highway. Basically, the police were looking for Haitians.

When I was traveling with my study abroad group, we never had any problems. The police officer would look inside the van and see the white people and say, "Pasa."

We never had to show any documents. Well, when we went to Dajabón, a northwestern Dominican city, my teacher allowed one of my American friends to go with us, who happened to be dark-skinned with an afro. Everything changed. At every "puesto de chequeo" we passed, they stopped our van. The security officer asked for everyone's identification. She had to pull out all types of documents to prove she was American and not Haitian. I could only surmise that the difference in treatment was because of the color of her skin and the style of her hair. However, playing devil's advocate, the Dominican Republic has a ton of Haitian migrants living there illegally and I suppose they were trying to protect their territory just as the United States does at its southern border. But, my white classmates could've also been living in the Dominican Republic illegally, so it appeared unfair that they only checked all of our documents when she was with us.

When it came to the Haitians, the discrimination was awful. It's one of the things I strongly disliked about the Dominican Republic. When riding in guaguas or public vans, they'd sometimes ride on the outside, hanging on for dear life. Many of the Haitian men would do it because they had no other way to get around. They often had the worst jobs: construction, maids, hair braiders and masseuses.

In both countries, the Dominican Republic and Colombia, it was a rare occasion that the socioeconomic classes mixed. In the Dominican

Republic, a third of the population lived in poverty so it wasn't as dramatic because there were more places where the poor congregated than the rich. In Colombia, where there were numerous wealthy families contrasted with an overwhelming amount of people living in poverty, the rift was dramatic. I met tons of poor people who were deafly afraid to go places that were outside of their socioeconomic class. It was to the extent that they were scared to step foot in a nice neighborhood and strictly only went there for work. They refused to go into a mall in a nice neighborhood. It was striking because in the States, at least in my experience, it seemed that more people freely went to public places, regardless of their socio-economic status.

Although being white certainly seemed to lead to better treatment and have its advantages in the Dominican Republic and Colombia, it had major disadvantages, too. Whiteness in their eyes almost always meant wealth. There was this assumption the darker skinned you were, the poorer you were, which meant if you were tan, brown or dark-skinned, the thieves usually left you alone, unless you were being obnoxious and speaking a ton of English in public, telling all of your business to strangers. On the other hand, white people were targets for crime.

They stood out in the Dominican Republic. Thieves assumed they had money because they were from Canada, Europe, or the United States. So many of them could not roam freely as I could because I blended in. From my recollection, they rode in taxies with drivers they knew or rode in groups; they weren't taking public cars and buses. And some of them got robbed. I never had a problem in the Dominican Republic, but in public, I also never spoke English, and I didn't walk around broadcasting my valuable things; no fancy jewelry and modest clothes. Also, men were drawn to the white women because they had white skin and blonde hair which was exotic to them. The white women had to be more selective on who they let into their circle.

In Colombia, Medellín and Bogotá specifically, it wasn't as bad for white foreigners because they were able to blend in more. There were more white Colombians. However, white Colombians were targets of thieves, too. The stakes were higher. Whereas in Dominican Republic, you might get robbed at knifepoint for your book bag containing your iPod (my friends did), in Colombia, you had to worry about getting kidnapped. The majority of my white Americans friends had their phones stolen at least once, either because they weren't paying attention or they were outright robbed.

To summarize, be aware of who you're going out with and how their skin tone is perceived in that society. Regardless of whether you agree with it, it's reality and you need to be prepared for situations that may arise. That way, you can handle it appropriately and not freak out and escalate the situation. If you're black hanging out with all white people, it's probably a good idea to bring another black friend if they're planning on going to ritzy clubs, just in case you can't get in and your white friends decide to leave you outside. If you're white, don't bring valuables with you and don't dress flashy if you're going to be out in public. Take extra security precautions. When I was out in public, especially by myself in large crowds, I kept English to a minimum.

Stephanie Claytor

Chapter 20:
Dominican-Haitian Relations

I love the Dominican Republic for its vibrant music and dance culture and welcoming people. Not to mention the active nightlife and beautiful beaches. It's always one big party there and you get the vibe as soon as you leave the airport. On the flip side, I disliked the mistreatment of Haitians that was prevalent in society and the negation of blackness.

I learned through conversations with Dominicans it was something that many were taught since childhood and would only be changed through dialogue, questioning the validity of their beliefs, and learning to appreciate their black heritage.

To understand the complex relations, you'd have to understand the history. First off, slaves were brought to both sides of the Hispaniola island, which now makes up Haiti and the Dominican Republic. According to historians, the French side of the island had thousands more, as the French turned it into a sugar production machine in the 1700s.

Less than two decades after the Haitian Revolution, Haiti took over the Dominican Republic. The Dominican Republic is the only country in the Western Hemisphere that got its freedom from Haiti, not a European power. Haiti ruled the entire island from 1822 to 1844. It was during this time some historians contend Haiti then turned into the enemy for Dominicans, and many wanted to do everything in their power to distinguish themselves from their island neighbor. Blackness was directly correlated with being Haitian. To separate themselves from Haitians, Dominicans began to think of themselves as Hispanic.

Later, Dominican dictator Rafael Trujillo, who ruled from 1930-1961, made it his business to whiten the Dominican Republic or as he called it, "blanquear la raza". He offered to accept up to 100,000 Jewish refugees during World War II to help develop the agriculture sector. Historical accounts indicate that about 1,000 came, and many settled in Sosua and the capital. Before that, historical accounts indicate that in 1937, he ordered his men to go to the frontier between the Dominican Republic and Haiti and kill any Haitian or Dominican who couldn't say "perejil" while rolling the 'r' correctly. That equated between 9,000 and 20,000 people being killed, according to historians. The massacre led to black people in the Dominican Republic doing whatever they could to conceal their blackness, so they wouldn't come off as Haitian. According to historian Henry Louis Gates, Trujillo, who had a Haitian grandmother, was able to unite the country by utilizing anti-Haitian sentiments.

Dominicans were psychologically and systematically taught from the ruling class to hate blackness. To avoid being called what Americans would consider black, the majority of Dominicans will refer to themselves as "indio" or Indian. Since the time of Trujillo, there's been a dynamic of Dominican preference and Haitian prejudice that is omnipresent in social life. Dark skin is almost always noted, and it's often stigmatized.

While I lived in Santiago, several Dominicans expressed to me they didn't like Haitians because they practiced Voodoo and spoke another language. But in reality, there were Haitians all around us who learned to speak Spanish, and some even spoke French and English. Many were Catholic. I befriended and studied with many who were well-off and enrolled in La Pontificia Universidad Católica Madre y Maestra, the Dominican Republic's most prestigious university. It seemed like the vast majority worked in construction, or cut sugarcane, or farmed or worked on the beaches or walked the streets selling ice cream. Many were simply there, working to provide a better life for their families, as many Dominicans fled to the United States to seek the same.

One day, I was walking to my favorite local bar, Frank's, in Santiago. When I arrived, everyone was quiet. I saw a cop on a motorcycle with a black man on the back of it. I asked the Dominican bar owner what happened. He said the Haitian guys came from around the corner with a bottle in their hand. Walking with bottles outside was commonplace in the Dominican Republic. He said the guy had stopped to talk to his friend when the police pulled up on a motorcycle and accused the Haitian guy of breaking into a house and stealing. He told the officer he didn't do it. The officer said he did do it and broke his bottle. Then, the officer demanded him to get on the back of this motorcycle so that he could transport him to the station. The guy wouldn't budge. The officer then shot his rifle up into the air. Then, the Haitian guy obliged. I was arriving as the shot was fired.

Terrified, my friends and I felt at such a loss. We asked his Haitian friend what we should do. We didn't have a car and didn't even know where the police station was. He called a Dominican friend and told him to go to the station. Luckily the officer actually did take the Haitian to

100

the station and the Dominican friend was able to get him out of trouble by paying for him to get out of jail. Now, of course I'll never know if the Haitian guy did break into the house, but the officer didn't provide any proof either. The way it was handled and the shooting into the air in the middle of an outside bar was unsettling.

Since I left in 2010, the situation has gotten worse. In 2013, the Dominican Republic Constitutional Court issued a decision to denationalize all Haitians with an irregular migratory status born in the Dominican Republic from 1929-2007. Anyone who didn't have at least one parent of Dominican blood was retroactively denied Dominican nationality. The United Nations Refugee Agency believes the ruling rendered approximately 250,000 residents of the Dominican Republic stateless, "a situation of statelessness of a magnitude never seen before in the Americas", according to the Inter-American Commission on Human Rights.

The United Nations Refugee Agency feared the ruling could create a human rights crisis, as it blocks those involved from receiving medical care, education and threatened deportation. The Inter-American Commission on Human Rights found the 2013 court case resulted in children and teens of Haitian descent born in the Dominican Republic being prevented from finishing high school and college, because they lacked a birth certificate or ID card. The practice of denying birth certificates to children born in the Dominican Republic to undocumented Haitian migrants is commonplace, according to the Pulitzer Center.

By rendering these individuals stateless and stripping them of their nationality, the Inter-American Commission on Human Rights said it took away many of their basic rights, such as the right for their children to go to school or college, the ability to contribute to social security, or obtain health service. It made it hard to find a good job and impossible to get married or divorced or register the birth of a child, or even open a bank account or secure a passport. It also impacted their ability to run or vote for public office or buy or sell property.

In response to the international outcry against the Constitutional Court's decision, Dominican President Danilo Medina passed a law in 2014, rendering the stateless people into two groups. Those who had a birth certificate were offered the ability to get it validated and have their nationality restored, as long as they were born between June 16, 1929 and April 18, 2017.

For the rest of the people affected who were born in the Dominican Republic but never received a birth certificate, they had 180 days to apply for a migrant status and after two years were offered the ability to apply for citizenship. The Dominican government told the Inter-American Commission on Human Rights that 8,755 people registered. The commission estimates there were 53,000 in this category.

According to Amnesty International, from August 2015 to July 2016, UNHCR, the UN refugee agency, verified 1,881 cases of Dominican-born individuals who had arrived in Haiti, voluntarily or following expulsions, and who were stateless or at risk of statelessness.

I contextualized this controversial relationship between these two nations, so that you're aware of what you're walking into when you decide to visit or move to the Dominican Republic. It's one thing to visit the resorts, but if you're actually living in the Dominican Republic and you have darker skin, it's a reality you will be confronted with. At first glance, Dominicans may confuse you for being Haitian and try to treat you differently. Always have a copy of your passport on you. And if you don't feel like arguing with them, a simple way to dispel their prejudice is to start speaking English. Their entire attitude will change.

Chapter 21:
The Path To Freedom

In contrast to the Dominican Republic, African heritage is celebrated in the Pacific coastal region of Colombia, similar to the United States. It's probably due to the influence of its large afro-descendant population that is fourth to United States and Brazil and Haiti in the Americas, according to many sources.

In Colombia, there's "Día de la Raza", a national holiday which Americans refer to as Columbus Day. For them, it's a holiday to recognize and protect the country's ethnic diversity and cultures. Living practically next door to the "Teatro Nacional", I got a rare treat on this holiday. I went to see the play, "Negrura Mia", which analyzed the history of Afro-Colombians. The play featured an all-black cast. It was powerful and I found it to be quite profound and insightful when it came to Colombian history.

After watching the play, I was shocked at the similarities between Afro-Colombian and African-American history. The play intrigued me to reflect upon our separate journeys and the present results.

The play, "Negrura Mia", focused on the current issues blacks faced living in Colombia and it reflected on the past. Each character tackled a different issue, including self-hatred, eroticism of the black body, exclusion from society, and the lack of answers for how blacks living in the country could remove themselves from poverty and live a better life.

One of the characters played an Aunt Jemima role, as she narrated the play. Her lines discussed how black women have always been la "gran teta" or big breast to Colombia because for years, they've been subjected to being maids and nannies, caring for the rich folks' children, always slaving in the kitchen. Then, she went further to say that that those who escaped the kitchen now worked on the beach, massaging the world for a few pesos.

The role of black women being world's nanny and cook is a collective history shared across the diaspora. In regions that are seen as touristic hotbeds, lots of black women have now become the globe's sex object and masseuse.

Another character in the play explored Cartagena, discussing how she was violated by a white French man, fascinated by her curvaceous, black body. During the play, she was enamored by him at first sight but then when he grabbed her butt as she served food, before she could even have a conversation with him, she became saddened because clearly he only saw her as a sex object. The eroticism of the black body originating during slavery, is still a serious issue today. European and American men flock to the beaches of Latin America to be with young, Latina women, mostly with tan and brown skin, who are willing to sell their bodies for an inexpensive price. Prostitution is legal in Colombia but it's limited to brothels in designated tolerance zones.

Beyond being seen as a sex object, this actress' lines also delved into exclusion. She tried to compete in the "Reina Nacional" or National Beauty Pageant, only to be denied because she was black. This section of the play reiterated how Colombian blacks have been excluded geographically and from national contests like the famous "Reina Nacional". It was not until 2001 that a black beauty queen won the contest, even though blacks make up a third of the population.

Another scene discussed the importance of positive black role models in a child's life. The message was delivered by an actress playing the character of a mother, whose son hated being black. She asked herself what she could do. Her son hated being black because every time he saw a black person, they were working in the kitchen, or in the fields, or as a security guard. They were never on television, and never doctors or lawyers. During her monologue, the actress said she knew there were black lawyers and doctors, but wondered where because she wanted to show them to her son so he would be proud of his black heritage. I've found this lack of professional black role models to be a serious issue in Colombia and Dominican Republic.

The play also emphasized the exclusion of blacks from Colombian society in the last scene, "Blackout". The scene featured a game where the actors asked the audience questions about famous Afro-Colombians who have been whitened or erased from Colombian history books, including Colombia's first and only black President, Juan Jose Nieto Gil, who served in the 19th century. The audience, full of mestizos, was silent throughout much of the scene, lacking the answers, so the actors told them they needed to read more.

This scene demonstrated that although much of Afro-Colombian history has been forgotten and watered down by the general population, Afro-Colombians have kept their story alive and passed it down to their children. I find this similar to my experience being African American.

Throughout the play, the kitchen manager represented the role of the slave plantation overseer: the Uncle Tom. He was the epitome of self-hatred. He was always mean to his employees (the other actors and actresses) and acted as if he had a higher social standing. Finally, he broke down and revealed that he hated his skin, and that his grandmother always told him to scrub his hands so they'd become lighter and to always be impeccable. He said all black people do is complain; instead, he preferred to watch the white man's behavior and learn. But in reality, during the play, he took advantage of the little power he had and abused his fellow black workers. He looked down on them instead of working with them to find a solution. He not only watched and learned, but he also hated himself because he realized he could never be white.

As I was sitting and listening intently to this play in Spanish, I was astonished that Afro-Colombians and African Americans have faced the same issues for decades. Both of us were forced to live in and integrate societies where we were not the dominant cultures. Perhaps the most important lesson from the play was what to do about the current state of black people living in Colombia; a question that no one seems to agree on.

Much of the play took place in the kitchen, a common place where black people congregate for work, socializing, and deriving solutions. As a symbol of running away from the serious issues Afro-Colombians face, a few of the actors left the kitchen. But the other actors remained. They said, "It's easy to leave…but to where?…the hardest thing to do is to stay."

This phrase is nothing further than the truth. There comes a time when a population of people cannot continue to run from their problems. Instead, they must become educated about the society they live in and rather than running away, they must fight and demand change. This is the state of the Afro-Colombian community. Although they liberated themselves way before many other slaves across the Americas and escaped to freedom, they are far from being free.

The struggle right now for this community is to come together as one unit regardless of what region they're from, class, or what color brown or black they are. They must work together to make changes in their communities and hold their government representatives accountable, along with supporting business owners who were born and raised in their communities, not people from other regions or countries who sometimes come to exploit them, and take all of their valuable resources. It is only when this happens that change, along with education, will take place. This is the "Negrura Mia" or blackness that each afro-descendant living in Colombia faces. And it's a similar reality that all afro-descendants across the globe have to deal with. "El camino a la libertad es duro y largo"… The walk to freedom is long and hard.

Chapter 22:
The Displaced

I found the disparity in wealth within the black Colombian community to be alarming and worse than in the United States. I met black Colombians who appeared to be very wealthy, who worked for the government, had traveled to Europe, studied in London, and had lived in the United States. When they returned to Colombia, and lived in let's say Bogotá, you would find them at the ritzy clubs, with a bottle or two of Aguardiente at their table, wearing the highest fashion, and donning the longest weave. They traveled around the city by taxi, never the bus or TransMilenio. They owned restaurants, were columnists for magazines, or worked for NGOs. The only thing they struggled with was English.

Then there were the displaced Black Colombians. You would see them outside in the nice neighborhoods alongside the indigenous selling fruits and shoes. They took the TransMilenio for two-to-four hours just to get them from the north side of Bogotá to the south side, transferring five times. Or better yet, they took ten buses to get to their destination. Sometimes their teeth were gone, and their body was visibly decaying because there was no money to go to the doctor. Clothes were used and shoes were worn down because there was no money to buy new, imported clothes. Their homes were sometimes unfinished with two rooms, a kitchen and a place to sleep barren because all they could afford was a mattress. No one would hire them because they lacked education, and English. The government promised to pay them every month, but the checks stopped coming a long time ago, or so they said. They were left to suffer in the capital city of Bogotá, living off of Kool-Aid, fish, rice, and beans. If they got a night out, it would be at the local bar where they would buy beer because Aguardiente, the country's liquor of choice, was equivalent to a week's worth of food. Do you get my drift?

This drastic gap in wealth within the Colombian black population was challenging for myself and my black colleagues to navigate. It was tough for us to make friends, being middle class African Americans. On many occasions, we didn't fit in with either group.

The displacement of afro-descendants is a serious issue. According to the United Nations High Commissioner of Refugees, as of 2016, more than 7.4 million people had been internally displaced in Colombia due to five decades of civil war; two million of those are estimated to be Afro-Colombian. And that's only since it started recording data on the topic. The organization attributed this to armed conflict in coastal and border provinces or states, such as Chocó, Nariño, Cordoba, and Putumayo.

Ironically, these provinces are heavily populated with indigenous and blacks, marginalized populations. They're also underdeveloped, and with little connection to the rest of the country. In some parts of these provinces, one can only get there safely by boat or plane. These areas also are rich in resources, such as gold and emeralds.

According to the agency's 2016 report, despite the government efforts to improve its response to forced displacement, widespread security risks and violence involving the forced recruitment of children and youth, sexual and gender-based violence (SGBV), threats, disappearances and murders, have continued.

According to teleSUR, statistics from 2015 show that 65.9 percent of the people from Chocó live below the poverty line and 37 percent are registered as living in extreme poverty. For five decades, Colombia has been in a Civil War with the Revolutionary Armed Forces of Colombia or FARC for short. People living near the Pacific coast have not only been caught in the crossfire of them but also paramilitary groups, and left-wing guerillas as they all fight each other and the government for territorial control. Targeted killings of those who spoke out against armed groups were common, as were mass displacements, forced recruitments and sexual abuse were all the norm, forcing many to flee their homes on the Pacific coast for Colombian cities.

After four years of negotiations, a peace agreement was signed between the Colombian government and the FARC, which went into effect in December of 2016. But even with the peace agreement, with the FARC fleeing the area, there are reports of new armed groups rising up to battle for control. Fighting for territorial control in the Colombian Pacific Coastal region among irregular armed groups has displaced 3,549 people from January to April of 2017.

To understand this situation better, I interviewed Bolo*, a displaced guy I met in Bogotá back in 2010. I met him in his barren apartment, full of concrete walls, where the mortar that held the bricks together seeped from the walls. He had nothing but an open room with a pallet to sleep on and a kitchen. The kitchen had a stove top, and a pipe that extended from the wall providing him water.

Bolo was from Barbacoas, in the Nariño province, located on the Pacific coast in the southwest part of Colombia. His town had about 35,000 people. Barbacoas is a historic town, founded in 1600. He said his town remained undeveloped and a hot spot for military groups because its leaders hadn't served it well. The military groups are also drawn there because it's rich in natural resources, such as gold and coca leaves, which contain cocaine.

Before the war with the FARC, Bolo said life was normal in Barbacoas. The people made a living off of agriculture and mining. The black culture was vibrant and beautiful. They didn't have much interaction with the rest of Colombia, because the Colombian government mainly focused on the central region of the country. But Bolo had to leave his home because he was a community leader and he said the violence caused by the armed groups in the region fighting over territorial control got so bad. He described massacres and murders happening often in his town, and military groups snatching people from their homes and killing them for no reason.

For him, leaving was hard, but he said he felt so vulnerable and unsafe that he had no other choice. The various armed groups had taken away all of his human rights. Living there, the violence got so bad he was afraid to leave his house to conduct daily errands. He decided to flee to Bogotá, even though it meant he had to leave behind the land his ancestors grew up on. The place where he'd spent the last 30 years of his life. He had to leave his wife and daughters and said it was a matter of *Do I want to die innocent, or do I want to live, even if it means being a displaced person in Bogotá?* He chose to leave town in a hurry and survive.

Bolo believed that most of Colombia had no idea what they were enduring in the southwest region of the country. He said the media rarely came there to cover what was going on. He had been living in Bogotá for two and a half years when I met him. He chose Bogotá because he heard there was work there, but he soon learned that statement was misleading.

"The work in Bogotá is not dignified. You can find a job as a security guard, or in a restaurant, or public works. These jobs are unstable. You work for a month and they get rid of you or the contract is done. You get paid minimum wage. Once, I went to work for an engineer for a month and he didn't want to pay me. They take advantage of you and disappear," Bolo explained.

To help the displaced adjust to the city life, Bolo said the government gave him ayuda monetaria. The money was to help pay for rent, food, clothes. He received 300,000 pesos ($103) once. He said he was supposed to get that check every three months, but in a year, he only received one check. He had no idea where the rest of his checks went. Bolo got help with housing from a nonprofit.

I mentioned to him the talk of the civil war with the FARC dying down in Colombia. He replied that the growing number of displaced demonstrates the war is far from over. This was 2011.

"Colombia will never change until it changes its pueblos. If the pueblos don't change and they remain with corruption, Colombia won't change," Bolo told me. As for his future, he said he's in search of stability. He also dreamed of opening a business. At the time, his focus was maintaining the basics: transportation, a home, food. He said he couldn't count on the government to help him.

He continually sought work and said he didn't want to settle for rebusque or the selling of any and everything on the street. He'd rather do things the honest way because he said Colombians associate the black man with rebusque, even though the majority of blacks like to work. Point in case, the phrase many rolos (people from Bogotá) used, "Me toca trabajar como negro", or "I have to work like a black man."

Through his daily struggle, Bolo believed blacks in Colombia always have and always will be discriminated against. In his case, he said the discrimination is even worse because he's displaced. He said it equates to Grupo Niche's "Han Cogido la Cosa" song that says "Blanco corriendo atleta negro corriendo ratero", which translates to "a white man running is an athlete, a black man running is a thief."

In May of 2017, the black population still living on the Pacific coast went on strike in Chocó and Buenaventura, protesting for better living conditions and an end to state-sanctioned violence. For years, the Colombian government has abandoned many of the afro-descendant and indigenous rural communities along the Pacific coast. They protested a lack of access to services, such as water, housing, health care, and education.

One of the reasons for the strike was the security crisis surrounding social activists, according to the Washington Office in Latin America. In 2016, the Office of the United Nations High Commissioner for Human Rights observed 59 killings and 41 human rights defenders had been killed in the first four months of 2017. One of those killings was of Bernardo Cuero Bravo of the Association for Internally Displaced Afro-Colombians, which the Washington Office on Latin America found concerning since he was denied on four separate protection measures after receiving death threats.

The Washington Office on Latin America also reported the initial Colombian government response to the protests was to violently repress and attack protestors, who were non-violent and included women, children and the elderly. The ombudsman's office reported 161 complaints of alleged police abuse during the protests, according to Human Rights Watch.

According to teleSUR, the 18-day strike in Quibdó forced the Colombian government to negotiate. Under the agreement, according to the newspaper El Tiempo, the Colombian government pledged to invest $150 million U.S. dollars in infrastructure projects and hospitals. Much of the money will be spent on paving the roads from Quibdó to Pereira and Quibdó to Medellín. When I visited Quibdó, the capital of Chocó, it didn't have a dependable direct highway between the two largest cities closest to it. The strike in Buenaventura ended on June 6, after a 20-day strike. The Colombian government pledged to invest $342 million in housing, infrastructure, health, public services, and access to justice, according to the Washington Office on Latin America.

It will be tough to find people like Bolo* who will sit and tell you what's really happening in society. Colombians, no matter what their circumstance, will want to portray the good qualities of Colombia to you. If you get the chance to talk to someone and have an honest conversation, ask them about how displacement has changed the country, and why people are selling things on the sidewalks and how the government cares for people who have been displaced. Ask them about their daily lives and you will find that they are dealing with hardships you could have never imagined. Read the newspaper. All of these things will give you a much better understanding of how things work, as well as the history of the country.

Stephanie Claytor

Chapter 23:
San Andrés

Because of my love for the Caribbean, there was no way I was leaving Colombia without going to its Caribbean island, San Andrés. I had never heard of it until I moved to Colombia, but everyone was telling me it was one place I had to visit before I left. I heard about the island during my first week in Colombia, when I saw the reggaeton artist from San Andrés, "Jiggy Drama," in concert singing "Chica Mala", on stage in Bogotá. I made up my mind then I was going to visit San Andrés.

If you love scuba diving, pristine blue waters, and few tourists, this is definitely the destination for you. It's a coral island and a part of the UNESCO Biosphere Reserve. Many consider it an exotic vacation destination.

While conducting some research about the island, I learned San Andrés was located in the Caribbean Sea, closer to Nicaragua than it was to Colombia. The archipelago is made up of San Andrés, Providencia, and Santa Catalina. San Andrés, the main island, is about 10 square miles and has a population of around 75,000 people. It is said the Dutch inhabited the island in the late 16th century, using it as a safe haven from pirates. The first real settlement didn't come until the early 1600s, when the British arrived. According to historians, the British came from Barbados and England and brought slaves with them from Jamaica. The Spanish occupied the island during the 18th century but the British retook it and made the three islands a colony. Then Simon Bolivar occupied the island and it officially became a part of Colombia around 1822. Now, the island is being transformed into an international holiday destination with hotels and resorts.

My quest to visit the island became easier when I met a woman named Leah* from San Andrés during a conference in November. She began to explain some of the issues the island faced. From her viewpoint, the native blacks who lived on the island were being discriminated against by the Colombians. Understanding the history, the only constant throughout so much change was the descendants of slaves who lived there. As the island transforms into an international tourist destination, she said life for the native blacks living there for centuries was changing for the worse.

Leah said her people, the native islanders, could not keep the island to themselves, away from the "Colombians" because they didn't have money or collateral. They lived on land passed down from their ancestors worth a fortune, but the Colombians were finding ways to take it away from them. She also said the police were constantly patrolling the islander areas, trying to find ways to put them behind bars. I knew this was a place I had to explore, another black Colombian community I had to get to know.

When I went, I decided to stay in Leah's home, so I could get a bird's-eye view of the islander life. When I got off of the plane, the feeling of paradise greeted me as I gazed at the blue water, and the fresh, humid air. A smiling black woman greeted me as I waited in line to leave the airport. I was surrounded by white Colombians going there with their families for holy week. I'm sure they assumed I was an islander going home.

As we drove through town to Leah's home, I saw a lot of unused land, which they called "bush" and homes. It seemed like she knew everybody and she greeted them as we passed by. Finally, we got to her house after a 15-minute ride from the airport. I could see the beautiful blue ocean and feel the breeze from her window. Her home reminded me of my home a little, though she hadn't finished it; the roof and the kitchen weren't done. She said they had to pay for it piece by piece and they didn't have the money.

As I walked outside in the back, I noticed a peculiar smell, and then saw the horse's butt from next door. I turned around and told her about the "interesting smell" and she laughed. Then, I smelled the marijuana coming from below, and said, "Very interesting."

I guess her neighbors lived below her for two years without a bathroom. They had two nicely painted two-room cabins and a bunch of chickens outside. I asked what all of the chickens were for and she said cock fighting.

The neighbor came over to drop off some crab soup. And while she was there, she was trying to eat up my friend's food. She had to be about six feet tall and weighed more than 200 pounds. That was all she talked about—food. Then she started dancing and whining, showing my friend's little daughter.

I began to learn the island dynamics. The natives from San Andrés referred to themselves as the cultural group "raizales," which is a creole-speaking, Afro-Caribbean ethnic group. For some reason, they felt comfortable speaking candidly about their situation to me, after they verified that I was not Colombian. We spoke in English.

Some were more disturbed than others. One told me it was an SOS, a call for help and that they wanted to speak to then President Barack Obama on the island's behalf. This was 2011. The people were upset that Colombia and its "panas" had taken over the island, and "Colombianized" it. They claimed that before the Colombians started to arrive, the people used to live the "quiet life". They were Christians and church-going people who raised their kids with morals and values, helped one another, and respected the land. Now, they said the drug trade had come to the island. Drug dealers used it as a launching pad to get the drugs to Mexico, the U.S. and Europe.

Also, the raizales blamed the Colombians for the growing violence and general craziness that had arrived. For example, the night before Easter, I was trying to be a good Christian and go to sleep at a reasonable hour, instead of going clubbing so I could make it to church on Easter. I assumed most islanders were doing the same. Well, below the hill, Colombians lived there. They were blasting music until about 3AM. It was so loud, I could not sleep. I could hear the lyrics to every reggaeton song they were playing. The homes were at the bottom of the hill, not next door. I began to understand their frustration because I could not sleep and was becoming irritated. I soon learned that anything that went wrong, the islanders blamed it on the Colombians.

Walking around the island, I saw the Malecón area full of duty-free stores to attract tourists. There was a nice tourist beach there, filled with non-islanders. I was told that most islanders refused to go to the beach. Most of the music heard there was in Spanish, mainly reggaeton, while the islanders listened to more reggae and gospel.

School was taught in Spanish and English; Creole wasn't taught. Most of the businesses operated in Spanish, even though the native islanders' first language was English and Creole. Only in islanders' neighborhoods, did they operate in English and Creole. According to statistics, islanders only accounted for 30% of the population, because back in the 1950s and onward, Colombia promoted migration to the island when it made it a free port and apparently, it worked.

Even the church services were conducted in Spanish and translated to English at the same time. Only the First Baptist church held on to its English tradition. Many of the islanders believed the government sent Colombians, but the worst ones, to inhabit the island. Ones who were not churchgoing, loud, poor, and ignorant, according to them. For example, they planned a J Balvin reggaeton concert on Holy Thursday, which my friend said was also disrespecting islander culture because they were having a concert on a sacred day.

It was obvious there was major division between the native raizales and the Colombians who lived on the island. Amongst the raizales, there were two different groups. Those who went along to get along, and those who staunchly opposed Colombianization. Those who went along to get along owned property near the ocean and rented it to tourists. The afro-centric militants in San Andrés wanted nothing to do with the newcomers. I went to their homes and churches for interviews and lunch. Some were more diplomatic with their speech than others. They were infuriated when I spoke Spanish in their homes, which was tough for me because when I saw palm trees, it triggered my Spanish. Up until then, I had only been to Spanish-speaking island destinations.

Before lunch, I interviewed one gentleman about the islander movement. In Creole English, he told me he'd shed blood if that's what it took to get the Colombians off the island. He told me to talk to President Obama, Amnesty International, or whoever in order to get the island help because basically, the Colombians had taken over the island and he wanted every single last one of them gone.

After the interview, I had lunch with his wife and him together. We ate crab soup out of traditional wooden bowls, accompanied by crab stew with pig legs—something I never ate before and seeing that my family ate extra healthy, I was about to die sitting there eating that pig fat. Of course, I smiled and ate it slowly.

Colombians, especially black ones, don't let food go uneaten. In my American mind, San Andrés was still Colombia because it legally was a province of Colombia and it had some cultural similarities, however, the raizales didn't see it that way. When I kept saying here, meaning Colombia, they had a fit! They kept saying *here* in San Andrés or *there* in Colombia because there's a difference. I couldn't help it.

I conducted my other interview with the church pastor. He spoke very eloquent English and his office was filled with English books, including one written by T.D. Jakes. He explained that San Andrés was having a movement to have more rights and more power in decision-making, especially over its natural resources and ecosystem. Right now, San Andrés is a department of Colombia, similar to a state. According to him, the islanders wanted to be either an independent nation or a sovereign territory of Colombia, like Puerto Rico.

Besides interviews, of course I had fun. One of the most rewarding experiences was visiting the "bush", which I learned meant "forest", where the islanders hung out away from the Colombians and where my friend's husband's family owned land. They had a sugar cane mill and sugar cane and made this dish called rondon in a wood-burning fire. Basically, they put fish and coconut milk, along with flour dumplings in this pot, sitting on coals on the ground, and cooked it. Meanwhile, the men went to go cut "caña" or sugar cane with their machetes, while the women sat and talked in hammocks, ducking from the fresh mangos falling off of the trees.

I filmed the men cutting sugar cane. They owned the land and were taking part in a family tradition. All of the men were voluntarily cutting the cane on their family farm so that they could eat it and drink its juice. It was a fun, family outing. Usually I associated sugar cane cutting with slavery or forced labor for low wages. To see this was extremely rewarding. And of course I ate all of the sugar cane on the ride home. You have to chew it and suck out the juice, then spit the cane out. It's addictive. I want some right now just thinking about it. There's so much to say about San Andrés but by the time I left, I decided it was one of my most rewarding trips thus far. I could even speak some Creole, and definitely understood it. If you decide to go, browse the touristy areas but definitely visit the islander part of the island near La Loma, as well as the First Baptist Church. And if you can, go with a native islander so you can enjoy the real experience of raizal life.

Stephanie Claytor

Section II

Now that I've shared some survival and cultural intricacies to be aware of before packing up and visiting or moving to Latin America, especially Colombia and Dominican Republic, I wanted to share highlights of some of the wonderful cities I visited. In this section of the book, I discuss places to visit across Latin America, especially if you would like to learn more about black culture.

Chapter 24:
Quibdó

Colombia's Pacific coast holds a special place in my heart, as evident within the original blog post I'm sharing with you, that I wrote after my first visit to Quibdó, the capital of Chocó, which is one of Colombia's majority black states:

Although many roads were not paved and stop lights were rare, you could feel the hospitality in the air. People sat outside with their families, while they blasted reggaeton music from the inside, so that the entire neighborhood could enjoy. A fried chicken restaurant existed on every corner. As we traveled through the downtown area, I noticed there was nothing but clothing stores and fruit and fish stands. Women flew by on motorcycles with their weaves, braids, and afros swaying in the air. At night, all of the young people headed to "La Zona Rosa" or the Red Zone to rumbear or party. During my first night, most people headed to see a salsa concert at Jennylao, a new nightclub in town that was one of the nicest I've seen in Colombia and definitely my favorite. It was amazing to me that the club was full on both levels, considering the fact that it cost $15 to get in and the cheapest bottle cost $45. That's expensive in Colombia, as a person who makes minimum wage earns $250 a month. I felt like I was in Atlanta! All of the women were divas, with their weaves right, short dresses, and stilettos.

The concert featured Ensamble Pacifico and it was excellent. While I was in Quibdó, I did not experience any blank stares like I did in Bogotá; all I felt was love.

In Quibdó, it seemed like the alcohol fell out of the ceiling because no matter whose house you visited, they offered you a beer, and then another, as if they had an endless supply. When you walked down the street with a native, you had to greet all of the neighbors as you walked by. When you visited someone's house, they would offer you dinner, whether it was something they cooked, or they'd fetch takeout, before you even told them you were hungry.

As a matter of fact, if they didn't know how to prepare what you asked for, such as warm oatmeal cereal, they would find a way to make it so that you were happy and add special spices to give it more flavor. When I met people, they told me they were happy to see me and asked me what they could do to help me enjoy my stay. This is what I call

Pacifico Hospitality, which in my mind is very similar to Southern Hospitality in the United States. I never felt so loved elsewhere in Colombia.

However, Quibdó was not all glitz and glam. It's definitely not a tourist resort. It's a modest city sitting on the Atrato River where the poor lived right next to well-off, and without suitable roads to travel to the rest of the country; the best way to get there is by air.

In Quibdó, there were definitely the haves and the have-nots. In the homes of the middle-class professionals where I stayed, they had huge flat screen TVs, SUVs, computers, big older homes with four bedrooms or more, internet, dogs, maids, and all of the other modern amenities that middle class families have. Those not as fortunate lived in four-room wooden homes set atop of sticks over muddy waters. This sector lived in extreme poverty with dirt roads, and little commerce. Many of these people were displaced from other towns in the province of Chocó due to violence. What struck me about Quibdó was its people's drive and motivation. While living in Colombia, the US Embassy offered my colleague and I the opportunity to give a presentation on American Black History in Quibdó. I decided to discuss the Civil Rights Movement and the changes in Federal laws that took place thereafter. I was ever so shocked when I arrived at La Universidad Tecnológica de Chocó, and there was a standing-room-only audience.

They were standing in a room with no air conditioning to hear us talk about a foreign country's dark history. I don't think it would be the same in the United States, or in other Colombian cities. There were so many questions that we could not answer them all.

When we arrived at the local public high school, there were 200 teenage students in uniforms sitting neatly in their chairs, quiet, and ready to hear what we had to say. Afterwards, they interviewed us, took pictures, and requested our autographs for their Afro-Colombian history posters as if we were celebrities. Many of them thanked me for coming because they said it's not often that black Americans visit their town.

It was this drive for knowledge that was quite impressive! In general, I found most middle-class Colombians to be well-read and educated, but I do not remember meeting one unintelligent person from Quibdó. The ones I met were all highly intelligent and, in some cases, were more updated about what was going on in the United States than I was at the time. Quibdó was not just an abandoned city full of displaced poor persons, although they made up around half of the population. The rest were lawyers, doctors, architects, professors, businessmen, accountants, scientists, and politicians.

If you want to feel welcomed, have intellectual debates, swim in crystal clear rainforest rivers, and dance to amazing salsa that has soul, go to Quibdó, un paraíso negro (a black paradise)!

That's just a glimpse of my first experience visiting the Pacific coast. The Pacíficos are people in Colombia who originate from the Pacific coast, including cities such as Quibdó, Buenaventura, Tumaco, etc. Many of their descendants now live in Cali and Medellín, due to displacement. When I went to Quibdó, I felt like I entered a black oasis. Every stereotype of American blacks you could think of was also present on the Pacific coast, except for the watermelons. I don't recall seeing those.

When I had conversations with Pacíficos, although it was in Spanish, it always felt like I was talking to my best friend from back home. It was like a long-lost deep connection. I guess because as black descendants, although thousands of miles apart, we shared the same struggles of dealing with the aftermath of colonialism.

When I talked to Pacíficos, they knew who Denzel Washington was. They admired former President Barack Obama and considered him their president, too. Many of them could even spit Jay-Z or Mary J. Blige lyrics, even though they didn't know what they meant.

What amazed me even more was their ability to preserve their heritage. They had their own dances and instruments, such as the marimba. They got their food from the rivers and ocean, and they had their own cuisine and recipes. Being on the Pacific coast was like visiting an entirely different country. Many of their homes were still made from bamboo stalks and wood.

From my understanding, Pacíficos are the descendants of slaves, who were brought to Colombia from Africa. These slaves escaped the ranchos outside of the cities, crossed the mountains and forest, and settled on the Pacific coast. The white ranchers, for the most part, never bothered to come find them. The Indians ran off through the rainforest, too. So, now when you go to the Pacific coast, you'll find the indigenous populations in the mountains, and blacks living near the waterways, and the coast; it's quite the combination. White Colombians are largely nowhere to be found, except for a few paisas (people from Medellín) who own businesses there.

In 1993, Ley 70 was passed to establish Afro-Colombians' rights to their own ancestral lands. With this law, if a community had lived there for a long period of time, it was determined to be their land and they were entitled to it. If the people were displaced from the land, it had to be returned to them. That's the short version. Although this law went into effect in the early 90s, it was just starting to get enforced when I was there in 2010, when the Colombian government was trying to negotiate a free trade deal with the United States, which mostly hinged on human rights advances amongst blacks and other marginalized groups.

That's not even half of the struggle Black Colombians endured. I believe that is why many of the Pacíficos were fans of black American culture. They did not try to erase their black culture by intentionally mixing with lighter skinned Colombians as some of the other black Latinos did in other countries. Instead, they preserved their culture. Like blacks in the United States, black Colombians, knew they were different and had a special culture. They fought for freedom from day one.

I definitely enjoyed my trip to Quibdó. It was a great way to explore Afro-Colombian culture. However, it's risky. On June 28, 2018, the U.S. Department of State issued a travel advisory telling people not to travel to the province of Chocó where Quibdó is located due to crime and terrorism. I made friends in Bogotá with people from there, so when I went, they housed me and took care of me so I didn't have any problems. I'd advise you to do the same.

Chapter 25:
San Basilio de Palenque

One of my favorite remote towns to visit in Colombia was San Basilio de Palenque. If you want to experience black culture in Colombia, you have to make a stop there. It made me feel like I was in a rural area on the continent of Africa more than it did South America. There were dirt roads, motorcycles, and animals wandering as they pleased. Everyone was black, dark-skinned, as if they had never mixed with anyone. It was located about an hour and a half bus ride southeast of Cartagena and had the historical pride of being the Americas' first freed slave town.

To get around, you better have some good walking shoes or un moto. Cars were practically non-existent. To get there, you had to go to the bus station at the southside of Cartagena and then take a bus. Then, you'd have to catch a moto into town. It's a secluded black oasis. You'll hear "champeta" music as soon as you get there; it sounds like island music and it's good for grinding and whining.

Being a light-skinned black person, I was an outsider. But my friends, one with dreadlocks and the other with beautiful dark Liberian skin, were like queens of the Palenque. All of the men smiled when we flew in on the back of motorcycles. Overall, everyone wanted to get to know us. A guy by the name of Jared* was my guide. He was born and raised in Palenque and attended college in Cartagena.

The Palenqueros are descendants of runaway slaves who escaped Cartagena, under the leadership of Benkos Biohó. He urged other slaves to flee, as well, and launched attacks on the Spanish. The Governor of Cartagena eventually signed a peace treaty with the group in 1605, which allocated a small section of the territory to Palenque. The Spaniards, then ruling Cartagena, violated the treaty in 1619 and captured Biohó. They hung and dismembered his body in 1621, spurring future distrust in government. Today, there's around 3,500 people who live in Palenque and it is a UNESCO World Heritage Site.

During my interview with Jared, he told me that Palenqueros, or people from Palenque, were raised in a different way, a rural lifestyle. He said that nobody messed with anyone. Parents could let their kids play outside freely without problems. Everyone in the neighborhood knew each other well enough to ask for favors. Jared's father said they lived in a different world that was tranquil. He believed they lived better because there wasn't much violence. They lived off of subsistence farming, where they survived on the produce they harvested, and spoke their native language, Palenquero. According to a UNESCO report, Palenquero is believed to be the only Creole language in Latin America with a lexical Spanish basis, and grammar related to the Bantu languages in Africa.

Jared said they didn't have social classes in Palenque, like in the rest of Colombia. He said they didn't differentiate who had a better quality of life and who didn't. There, money was needed for some superficial things, but it wasn't the priority. Jared's father said in Spanish during my interview that at one point, many people in the town didn't want to learn how to read or write because they didn't want to learn bad customs.

"The older generation didn't force their kids to go to study, because they would bring the bad examples here," said Jared's father during my interview.

But in the late 1990s and 2000s, things changed.

"Here has changed because now we don't use water from the aqueduct. Instead, we use water from the tube," he continued.

During this time, the younger generation started to receive scholarships designated for afro-descendants to attend universities in the city. This has created mixed emotions amongst the elders who do not want these new intellectuals to come back and change Palenque.

"The people want to change our attitudes here but that shouldn't be changed," Jared's father explained.

Jared said when he went to college, with the rest of the costeños, he felt bad sometimes. He described how he left Palenque to live in Cartagena and saw how others lived, how they had things and went out on Sundays to eat ice cream or go to the movies. He said it changed his social life. He'd change his accent because the kids laughed and made fun of him. Jared spoke Spanish slower because it wasn't his first language, similar to a person from Tennessee with a southern accent moving to Boston.

Nowadays, there's an estimated 20,000 Palenqueros that live in nearby cities, some living as far away as Venezuela. Jared said many returned only for vacation. According to him, there was a trend of Palenqueros leaving and not returning because of the living conditions. Additionally, there wasn't permanent or stable employment in Palenque. I didn't see any restaurants or shopping malls. Just corner stores and takeout places, and a small nightclub.

My first night there, we were unsure if we could get back, and Jared's dad offered to let us stay at his house, but I looked around. The floor was concrete. There was an outhouse, pigs running around outside and dogs coming in and out as they pleased.

Jared lived with his father and several brothers. I don't remember why but his mother wasn't there. It was a two-to-three room house full of men. I was there to experience the elements and understand their way of life. The cold water in Cartagena was enough of a culture shock for me. I decided not to stay overnight. We left on the last bus out of town. I returned several more times because I loved the beauty of this black community—so in tune with nature and living off of the land.

If you visit, either go with someone who is from there and spend time with their family, or take one of the tours that leave from Cartagena. The people there are very friendly and it's definitely worth the trip. In October, they host the annual drum festival where guests can take drumming classes or learn about the traditional Palenque hairstyles or learn the basics of the language. There are also concerts throughout the night, playing the traditional Palenquero music. The festival is usually four days of partying, celebrating Palenque culture.

Chapter 26:
Cali

Cali, Colombia, is located about three hours from the Pacific Coast in La Valle del Cauca. It is the third largest city in Colombia and known as the World's Salsa Capital. It is also famous for its plastic surgery centers and active nightlife.

This is why Caleños are prideful. The saying goes, "Cali es Cali...los demás es lomas," which means, "Cali is Cali and everything else in Colombia is mountains." After several visits there, I'd have to say that's partially true.

Cali may have la mejor rumba or the best parties/nightlife in Colombia, but that's only if you go out in mixed groups with girls and guys. If you go out with a group of girls, like we did, you can forget about dancing salsa. In Cali (and in many instances in Bogotá), people go out in groups with people they know and they dance the entire night together. A lot of men do not ask women they do not know to dance because they are unsure if the woman has a boyfriend, husband, etc. If a man does ask a woman to dance, whom she has never met, in many cases, the woman would say *no* because she didn't know the man or trust him. At least that's what the Colombians told me. This was very difficult for us Americans to grasp. Meeting guys in the club just did not appear to be the Colombian way. Usually, you had to be introduced to someone.

Another lesson we learned was "no tengo plata" means "I do not have any money" and when the bill comes, "I am not going to chip in." From an American standpoint, when someone says, "I'm broke" or "I don't have any money", that means they want to go somewhere cheap where they will spend less. Not in Colombia. It literally means, *I have zero pesos to spend*. We learned this the hard way when we went out with some Colombian guys and they did not contribute to the bill. Essentially, we learned it's always better to clarify things when money is involved because although something may be translated, that doesn't mean it has the same meaning within the two different cultures. From my experience, men often paid for the entire date early on in the relationship. So, if they did not have any money, they would not go on a date. Usually they were too embarrassed to admit they were broke so they would make a million excuses as to why they couldn't go out. Beyond these valuable cultural lessons, I had a lot of fun there.

I enjoyed staying at the Iguana Hostel. It was super cheap, clean and secure and it had hot water. It was located in a convenient part of town near restaurants and stores and it was easy to get to the center of town. You'll definitely want to check out the San Antonio neighborhood. It's the colonial section of town. It had cute coffee shops and it's a nice place to meet up with friends.

My favorite day trip was to San Cipriano. This was a quaint Afro-Colombian town about two hours from Cali, along the river. There, people used wooden motorized carts along a railroad as the main mode of transportation which I found fascinating. Many tourists visited there to go swimming or tubing in the river. The water was clean, clear, and cold; perfect for hot sunny days. The locals were friendly and seemed to be used to foreigners visiting. We stopped to play dominoes with some miners living in the area. Also, there were numerous Colombian soldiers from the National Army stationed there, so we didn't feel unsafe.

If you're visiting Cali, the best time to go is December 25-30 for "La Feria" (The Cali Fair). It's one of the most important cultural events in Cali, celebrating the region's identity with its salsa marathon and dance parties.

If traveling around the holidays isn't your thing, I'd recommend going to Cali's "Festival Mundial de Salsa (The World's Salsa Festival)". It was truly an amazing experience! The costumes were fabulous and the dancing was impeccable. Colombians dance salsa quite differently from everyone else. Their style can be identified by the way they quickly move their feet to the beat. On the other hand, Puerto Rican and Cuban salsa involves more turns. Also, Colombian salsa has more of a Samba influence, perhaps because of Colombia's close proximity to Brazil.

Many of the older dancers I interviewed told me salsa had given them the opportunity to travel and perform in other countries, such as Spain, Great Britain, and the United States. They'd won prizes in Las Vegas and all of them dreamed of becoming internationally known professional dancers. To put it simply, salsa changed their lives; they lived, breathed, and depended on it.

It was common for children in Cali to learn salsa from the time they could walk. There were three-year-olds on stage dancing and being flipped across the floor. Salsa was equivalent to hip hop for caleños! Basically, children enrolled in salsa schools when they were young.

Many grew up with the dream of becoming professional dancers. And for many, it was their way out.

The World Salsa Festival was their chance to show off. And boy did they! The costumes were so elaborate and dazzling. Fake eyelashes, metallic makeup, hair pieces, leotards, and salsa heels were some of the accessories I noticed. The men wore glittery suits. The kids looked so cute with their partners. All of the different salsa schools got on stage and the performers moved their feet a mile a minute. Teams from other countries came, as well. There was one Japanese team competing and another couple from Puerto Rico.

When the festival first started, the entire outdoor coliseum had to get up and sing the national anthem. Everyone stood, but it seemed like hardly anyone was singing. Then, when the caleño anthem came on (state anthem), everyone shouted and jumped to the song. That's when my friends and I realized how regionalized Colombia was. People were far more proud of their state than their country.

If you go to Cali, make sure to dance salsa in Juanchito, and climb the mountain to see El Cristo Rey. Another good time to visit is during the Petronio Alvarez Festival. It is the biggest celebration of Afro-Colombian and Pacific culture in the country held every year in August, a celebration of music, food, drink, and culture. And catch the "Mio" around the city, which is Cali's version of the TransMilenio.

Stephanie Claytor

Chapter 27:
Samaná

In the Dominican Republic, located on the country's northern coast in between Punta Cana and Puerto Plata, a beautiful city and region that has a past that's not well-known to the outside world is Samaná. When you get there, you will notice a lot of the people have last names in English, and some even speak English. That's because Samaná is where thousands of freed black American slaves immigrated to in 1824 in search of a better life, back when the Dominican Republic was ruled by Haiti.

According to Martha Leticia Willmore, a local historian there, the Haitian president back then invited freed slaves living in Philadelphia to move to the island, with the promise that the Haitian government would provide them land. The Haitians hoped the slaves would influence the area with its culture and civilized way of living, according to Willmore.

It was during a time in the United States where freed slaves faced the daily fear of being kidnapped and sold back into slavery and also, feared the American Colonization Society would send them back to Africa. In the American Colonization Society's annual report, dating back to 1824, the society estimated that all 200,000 freed blacks could be sent back to Africa within the next 50 years. It was under these circumstances and these constant threats that compelled more than 6,600 freed blacks to immigrate to Hayti or what's now Haiti and the Dominican Republic, according to Willmore. Many of them attended Mother Bethel AME Church in Philadelphia, under the direction of Richard Allen, the founder of the African Methodist Episcopal (AME) Church.

"Sometimes I cry. If it wasn't for the bad treatment of blacks back then, we wouldn't be here in the Dominican Republic. We would be there," said Ambrosia Mejia Shepard in Spanish, during my YouTube documentary, African American Descendants Living in Samana, Dominican Republic Pt. 1. Back in 2009, she ran a small motel on the bay in Samaná. She said she was a fourth-generation African-American descendant.

The elders told Willmore the voyage took three months for some. She said they brought along with them 33 last names, including

Johnson, Vanderhorst, Kelly, King, Rodney, Sidney, James, Mitchell, Hamilton, Green, Barret.

"When they came, they brought their soils with them and they soon built nice homes," Willmore said during an interview for my documentary.

"When they came, they brought teachers, so they had schools and they had training for children."

When the kids finished school, Willmore said their parents sent them back to the United States for college, paid for by the money they made from their cacao fields. She said they then returned as professionals. But that has since changed.

"When the price fell, and they didn't buy from here anymore, the people began to cut down their fields. And when the price come back again, long years after, they didn't have it," Willmore explained.

Without the profits to fund the American education, she said most of the families sent their kids to Dominican universities nowadays. Willmore said early on, the parents didn't want their children marrying the Dominicans and Haitians. Eventually, they began to marry outside of their cultural group.

"When they mix, they fall out and leave the good part behind," said Willmore shaking her head.

Willmore missed the old days when the young people used to sail. She said that's rare now because they're not building as many boats.

In schools in Samaná and the rest of the Dominican Republic, Spanish is now the primary language. Basic English is taught in Samaná as a second language. Before, most of the population was African-American descendants. In 2009, Willmore estimated they consumed about 40 percent of the Samaná population.

"30 percent of the people in Samaná speak English because they miss the English. But our English language is in the past. Today, we don't speak great English like we should speak it because we speak more Spanish than English," said Santiago Willmore, a guide in Samaná and also an African-American descendant.

"I have to speak English in my home. Then when I'm out with my friends, I have to speak Spanish," said Mejia-Shepard.

Mejia-Shepard shared that a lot of the customs have disappeared, too. When she grew up, she said the elders would punish the children if they said a bad word in front of them. Now, she claimed the kids said bad words in front of the adults and didn't feel ashamed as they did in her generation. She said the younger generation lacked respect.

"When I was little, my first language was English until I was six or seven years. When I moved with my mom and dad, I stopped speaking English and I started speaking more Spanish, the language that is more dominant here," said Clayton Diaz Hidalgo, a sixth generation African-American descendant, and one of the many people I interviewed on camera while there.

Clayton Diaz Hidalgo also remembered his ancestors as respectful people who taught their children to respect their elders, go to church and consult with God on everything. He admitted he wasn't doing those things.

Others admitted they had lost a lot of the culture and didn't value the English language. They said the culture gets passed down in the food and desserts.

"The problem is the customs that we had before are lacking. We have assimilated so much that we now speak Spanish. Now the elders don't understand English very well because they forgot it," said Santiago Willmore.

"My grandfather, he knocked me if I come and speak Spanish. He say I'm not Spanish. I'm English. Speak to me in English," Mejia Shepard said.

"But if I go to New York, I'm considered Dominican. They're not going to consider that I come from African-American descendants. But I feel American just as any other American. Why can't I go to the United States? I come from two Americans," Mejia Shepard questioned, frustrated over the matter.

The cultural shift is also evident during their church service. While a sign written in English hung above the pulpit with the popular religious phrase, "Glory to God in the Highest", the church services and songs were conducted in Spanish. The pastor preached in Spanish, but the service felt like a traditional African-American Baptist church service. After nearly every phrase the pastor said, congregants could be heard saying, "Amen."

Then a woman started shouting from her pew, "Tu está con nosotros," or "You are here with us," and "Tu estas con nuestro pueblo" or "You are here with this town," as everyone said "Amen." It was intriguing to see the similarities as I looked around at the brown and dark brown faces in the room.

The area is also becoming a big tourist attraction in the Dominican Republic. One resort is on the bay of Samaná, and another is on an island nearby. Many of the locals sell artwork or use their boats to transport tourists back and forth.

"Everything lost now. Change," said Mejia Shepherd.

"The young people gain their money. And they drink it, gamble, and all that," said Willmore. "Many of the young people, when they know that land is theirs, they are selling it."

Willmore was upset about the situation because the farms were what her ancestors survived on. She said they didn't appreciate the land that was passed down to them.

"The old people left it for them and they are doing what they feel like," Willmore said.

Meanwhile Mejia Shepard said her family was busy reclaiming their father's land. He came over from the United States and she said he bought the land legally. She found all of the paperwork. She said she felt like an immigrant and more African American than anything.

I stumbled upon Martha Willmore's story while studying abroad in the Dominican Republic in 2008. She was one of the stops on our bi-monthly trips around the country. I found her story so intriguing, I returned the following spring to shoot my documentary for my college honors thesis project.

I went back to the country in 2012 and stopped by Samaná searching for her, hoping she was still alive. I knew she was in her eighties. After asking around for the elderly black woman who spoke English, town folk took me right to her home. She seemed to have aged a bit and was frail, but she still had her memory. I recently learned she was featured in the New York Times in December of 2018.

Besides learning about this somewhat untold, forgotten history, Samaná is also known for whale-watching in the Bahia de Samaná. I wouldn't recommend it. It involves hopping on a boat with strangers for four hours in the middle of the ocean. The most you will see is the whale spout water or flip up its tail out of the water. Meanwhile, by the end of the four hours, everyone was puking. I didn't vomit but after the first hour, even with a dose of Dramamine, I felt nauseous. My stomach kept turning and I spent most of the trip in the bathroom. That was after one of the boat operators told me he would not take me back to shore and I had to wait until the trip ended.

I'd recommend visiting Las Terrenas, which is turning into quite the resort and beach town and is known as the perfect expat beach haven to some. It has restaurants and a nightclub that had a lively salsa night. A lot of Europeans hang out there, mainly French, Italians, Brits and Germans. The beaches were beautiful when I went there in 2012. They felt very private and weren't nearly as populated as Punta Cana or Puerto Plata. I got there by driving a rental car from the airport in Santo Domingo to Samaná, and then to Las Terranas. They had just built the new highway so it was a fairly easy ride and the highway there wasn't too populated. I stayed at Hotel Alisei which had gourmet food and the spa was marvelous! I'd definitely recommend the hot stone massage. The hotel is right across from the beach. It's very affordable with rooms, averaging $120 a night, depending on the time of year. The room rates drop below $100 in September and October.

Overall, I'm fascinated by the history of Samaná. Had I never studied abroad in the Dominican Republic, I would've never known this important piece of black history. The trip there just reaffirmed how important it was to travel and learn the history on my own instead of relying on what I was taught in school.

Stephanie Claytor

Chapter 28:
Quito

After nine months of meandering the bustling streets of Bogotá, I was given the opportunity to take a reprieve in Quito, Ecuador, with my fellow English teacher colleagues. Our program included an all-expense paid trip there for six days.

During the seminar, we met with our superiors to discuss and come up with strategies to better serve our students in the areas of vocabulary, pronunciation, games, and interactive activities.

Later on in the week, we went to a local school to test the new English teaching strategies we learned. The seminar also served as a space where we met American English teachers from Colombia, Peru, Ecuador, and Venezuela. We all got to know one another better and had a good time while visiting Ecuador.

I didn't know what to expect about Ecuador. All I knew beforehand was that it had a greater indigenous presence and a black population that lived in the Esmeraldas region. I decided to extend my trip for three days, so I could visit the Esmeraldas region, since my goal had always been to learn about as many black populations living in the Americas as possible.

When I arrived in Quito, I was impressed. The airport was newer than Bogotá's or at least it appeared to be. The customs line was short and things were orderly. I noticed that the men had more "swag" or should I say urban style, because there were a few of them waiting and they had on white tees, and baseball caps. Now, since I am older, that wasn't my image of an ideal man, but at least it was a step in the right direction and far better than those Bogotáno long hair Mohawk haircuts that were not attractive to me.

When we got on the bus, the folksy bachata blues caressed the lobes of my ears. *Finally, some good music,* I thought. I was tired of hearing vallenato all day and night in Bogotá. As we traveled to our hotel, I noticed that Quito looked just like Bogotá but without the chaos. It was cloudy, rainy, and chilly, in the fifties, requiring a jacket. The temperatures there rarely dipped below 44 degrees or above 70 degrees.

The city was mountainous with concrete plain colored buildings everywhere. They even had a TransMilenio like Bogotá. But I wondered where were all of the beggars? The people selling stuff on the street, the endless pedestrians? After living in Bogotá for so long, that was a

139

normal sight to me. I only saw a few during our 20-minute ride to the hotel. It felt like it was a ghost town.

After being there a couple days, I noticed a few things. The people seemed to be friendlier and more down to earth. The women didn't dress in stilettos and wear shirts with cleavage just to go to work. And the women also didn't wear a lot of makeup. It didn't appear they indulged in plastic surgery as much as Colombian women either. They were normal people living life.

There was also a greater American presence. Ecuador uses American dollars as its currency and has since 2000. The designs of the dollar bills are identical to the United States currency, except some Ecuadorian coins have images of Ecuadorian leaders instead of past American presidents. When I was in Quito in 2011, everything was super cheap. I also saw American businesses, such as Quiznos and workout centers like Curves.

It was amazing to me that at 8AM on a weekday, the streets were almost vacant. Did people work? There were hardly any cars on the streets either. Where were all of the trancones or traffic jams that paralyzed Bogotá. The city was amazingly calm, and quiet, and it was the capital.

I could see why so many American universities sent their students there to learn Spanish. Although the state department issued security warnings concerning the country off and on, I felt completely safe there and the people's Spanish was so much more understandable. They used basic words that were transferable across the Spanish-speaking world, yet in a clear manner, not like in the Caribbean where the Spanish was what I like to call "chopped and screwed" or in Colombia where they used a more advanced, formal version of Spanish and had their own vocabulary.

The food was so much better. The drinking water wasn't safe there, so I had to make sure they used good water for my ice and drinks. Overall, the food didn't upset my stomach. They had delicious shrimp ceviches with a spicy orange sauce and served bread with restaurant meals, which was an American staple that I was glad to see reappear.

In the hotel, I was surprised to see the cable had Aljazeera English. Also, the hotel rooms had carpet, similar to an American hotel. When we ate breakfast, I noticed another thing: Quito had an Asian presence. There were many Asians visiting. That was something that was almost as rare as snow in Bogotá or the rest of Colombia.

During my initial observations, I remained impressed. Then, we went on a cultural tour and my opinion shifted. It was a tour of the historic Catholic churches in Quito, but it turned into a look at how the Spanish Catholic Priests "civilized" the Indians and Blacks, whom they believed didn't have a soul and were connected to the devil. We saw a massive painting of "hell" hanging on the wall in one of the churches. It showed white bodies being possessed by black creatures that were part human, part ape. I was prohibited from taking a picture of the painting but it was quite disturbing since on another wall, there was a painting of heaven and I did not see any black figures in that one, just white bodies. In every church, all of the saints and figures, including the Virgin Mary, were white—extremely white with blue eyes. I found this problematic because according to my upbringing in the church, this was not how the Virgin Mary looked. The icing on the cake: the tour guide said the Virgin Mary was rumored as being "the prettiest woman in Quito."

After 30 minutes of this "cultural tour", I had heard enough. However, I did enjoy the architecture in "el Centro" or downtown Quito. Its historic district was much nicer and cleaner than Bogotá's. The buildings were very well taken care of, restored, and beautiful.

Some other highlights of the trip were our resort stay in Arasha, a rain forest resort with cabana or cabin rooms, a swimming pool, Jacuzzi, hot water, river, nightclub, and "Negrito beach", in which one of the employees could not explain why it was named that way because the sand wasn't black.

Our trip to Esmeraldas ended up being a bust. We took a seven-hour bus ride to get there. That allowed us to see most of Ecuador. We were traveling northwest of Quito and it seemed to be underdeveloped. When we got there at 11PM, everyone we came across appeared to be drunk and there were a lot of men in the streets, running around and trying to make advances toward us. It was just an environment that was questionable for two young pretty girls to be in, not knowing the area, culture and its customs.

When we checked into our hotel room, I saw this humongous Dominican sized cockroach. Then, we saw another one. I could not sleep and I was traumatized. So, with the accumulation of my friend feeling unsafe and me traumatized by the roaches, we left out of there running the next morning back to Quito.

If you visit Quito, explore Old Town and take a tour so you can hear the history for yourself. Visit the churches and check out Calle de la Ronda, a great spot for pictures lined with shops, cafes and art galleries. And don't leave without taking a short trip to the outskirts of Quito to stand on the equator.

Chapter 29:
Cartagena

In an effort to witness Colombia's National Beauty Pageant, otherwise known as the "Concurso Reina Nacional", I headed to Cartagena de las Indias at the beginning of November. This famous city, located on Colombia's Caribbean coast, is the nation's tourism capital. Known for its romantic appeal, the city was beautiful, with blistering sunny weather, pretty beaches, and Spanish colonial architecture.

Well, that was the tourist district also known as Boca Grande and El Centro. I had a different experience. I stayed with my fellow English-teaching colleagues in Mar Bella, near El Centro. The Reina Nacional was an eight-day festival for Cartageneros (people from Cartagena) which meant no work and all play.

When I say play, I mean parades of people running through the streets with shaving cream and spraying it at anyone who walked by. Or throwing water and eggs from balconies at passersby because they're too good to be on the streets with the locals. And when the parade was over, the teenage boys began to throw fireworks at each other, and the crowds behind them, while blasting reggaeton music for four hours straight.

These were the things I witnessed. Yes, we threw some "espuma" or shaving cream at people on our way back from lunch, but the fireworks, absolutely not. Since when was it OK to literally throw fireworks into a crowd of people? It was so bad, we had to run for our lives into our apartment, because they were conveniently playing with fire right outside of my friend's front door.

Besides those experiences, there were many other things that made Cartagena different from other Colombian cities. The first thing I noticed was that almost everyone was brown. I felt like I was back in the Dominican Republic.

The music was different. We found a club called Green Boon in a neighborhood called "La Castellana". There, they played a mixture of reggae, reggaeton, electronica, merengue, bachata, and salsa. Again, I felt like I was back in the Caribbean, enjoying myself. Primarily, riding around the city in busetas or buses, I noticed the stark class difference. There were a few upper-class neighborhoods, the tourist district, and then the barrios. I didn't see a large middle-class presence.

Unlike the other cities, I saw gringo tourists everywhere, mostly white men. In the centro, there was one club my fellow African-American colleagues said they were not permitted to enter and were told the typical bouncer excuse: "It's a private party." My friends said clearly it wasn't a private party because the bouncer allowed their white American and mestizo rich Colombian friends to enter right in front of them.

Other than that, the city was a great place to visit. I thoroughly enjoyed the seafood meals topped off with coco lemonade, historical attractions, visiting the palenques (runaway slave communities), and champeta music.

The city really turns into something special on New Year's Eve. The restaurants put tables in the streets, in the walled section of Cartagena or "El Centro". Everyone wore white and ate dinner in the streets. Then they counted down to the New Year together and popped champagne when it arrived. The salsa music started blaring and the party began.

My New Year's Eve there was like no other. After some fine dining, my friends and I met up with a group of people outside the walled city at a hostel. Inside, was a large group of guys from Brazil, folks from Australia, and folks from Ireland. We all drank some beers and prepared to celebrate. These were complete strangers by the way. Next thing I knew, we were running across the street and entering the walled city like a herd. We all continued to run through the streets of "El Centro", at full speed, screaming, "Happy New Year" in three different languages: Spanish, English, and Portuguese. The Colombians were sitting at their dinner tables looking at us like we were crazy. The Brazilians had a huge flag with them, big enough to completely cover three of us and they were waving it as we ran through the streets. Then, one of the Brazilians decided to get on top of a table and scream "Happy New Year" in Portuguese, along with whatever else. He fell off of the table and as he tried to get down, he came crashing down onto my big toe. But that didn't stop me. We kept on running through the streets until the countdown. After that, we popped champagne, danced and then headed to one of the ritzy clubs to finish the night. I have no idea why we were running through the streets, but it was one of the best New Year's Eves I've ever had. And what better way to bring in the New Year at age 22.

If you're going to Cartagena, stay in a boutique hotel. Explore the walled city and stop by the Castillo de San Felipe de Barajas. Head to Playa Blanca on Baru island. Party on a chiva. Check out the nightclubs and eat ceviche and coconut rice. And before you leave, head to El Totumo volcano, and have a mud bath in an active volcano.

Stephanie Claytor

Chapter 30:
Carnival

Barranquilla's Carnival is one of the most popular carnivals in the world. Many Colombians flock to Barranquilla to join the festivities. It starts the Saturday before Ash Wednesday and continues through Tuesday. Daily, there are parades and every night, there are concerts in the streets, all across the city, and drunken people everywhere.

My American English-teaching colleagues and I rented two apartments and we all went together. Every night, there were parties in the streets and it was a lot of fun. There were tons of concerts; it was hard to choose which one to go to.

The first day, being cheap, we went to the parade. We didn't purchase the bleacher seats so we were unable to sit and had to stand in the streets. There were so many people, we couldn't see the parade. Instead, we spent the afternoon avoiding getting squirted with foam, to the point that one loses visibility. What is it with Latin America, carnival, and people attacking each other? In Dominican Republic, it was smacking each other on the butt with fabric covered balls, to the point of leaving bruises; in Colombia, it was squirting foam at each other until they were covered in it.

The following day, we attended the grand parade. We sat in the bleachers and enjoyed a fantastic view. The bleachers were set up on both sides of the street, allowing people to order liquor and food in their seats. I'll give the Colombians credit—there were hundreds of dance groups participating. It took longer than two hours to see each group pass by where we were sitting. Before then, I had never seen anything like it. The dancers had on unique colorful, gorgeous costumes, and most could dance well and presented entertaining performances. It was evident the participants had practiced their routines for months.

What I didn't like were the several dance groups of young boys, dressed in black face. They painted themselves in black paint, including their faces, and their lips in red lipstick and made bug eyes. Then, they ran in circles for the crowd, acting like zombies. The boys were shirtless, barefoot and wearing ripped jeans. They looked like homeless people or savages. It was even more upsetting to see the crowd laughing at them, as if their behavior was entertaining.

When I asked a Colombian what they were supposed to represent and why the young boys were acting like that, the Colombian stranger replied that the black-faced boys were representing African culture, and slavery. Apparently, this is one of the characters and dances featured in the carnival every year, called the "El son de Negro." That's when I lost a lot of respect for Barranquilla's carnival. Those boys are an image I was never able to erase from my mind. This is what they taught their children about African culture? The boys looked like clowns and I felt they were making fun of African culture. It certainly wasn't a flattering representation and myself being of African-American descent, I was highly offended. What was more upsetting was that the parents of these boys allowed their children to do something like that. It was a disgrace. I was glad that my white American colleagues also felt it was disturbing.

To make matters worse, when I returned to the airport in Barranquilla, there was a cardboard image of "El son de Negro" that every passenger was forced to pass on their way to boarding the plane. While I was disgusted, I was not quite surprised. Many of the slaves entered Colombia through Cartagena. Therefore, many of the people on the northern coast of Colombia have some form of African heritage. Yet, many of those costeños often negated that heritage.

If you plan to go to carnival, book early because the hotels often sell out. Spend the cash and get the bleacher seats for the parades. You will enjoy your experience more. Research carnival beforehand because there's a lot of folklore involved and you'll want to understand what's happening in the parade in front of you. And prepare to get messy because you're bound to leave covered in foam.

Reflections

Overall, Colombia and Dominican Republic are captivating countries with plenty to offer. I'd recommend living in either one of them for a life-changing experience; you will grow immensely. Your Spanish will, too.

From an American perspective, both will challenge you. You will learn how to not be so naïve. The Colombian concept of "No dar papaya", has never left me. I'm always thinking about if I'm doing something that will give someone an opportunity to steal from me and how I can better protect myself and my belongings. I learned how to be proactive in protecting myself.

The Dominican Republic will teach you how to bargain. There, the price for everything was up for negotiation. I took that skill home with me; I'm always asking about the discount.

In Colombia, there's always a festival or holiday and reason to celebrate. In the Dominican Republic, the clubs are open daily. There's not an hour of quietness on the street. The bachata and merengue music are always nearby.

Both countries are just a lot of fun overall and I recommend everyone live abroad for a few months, at least once in their lives.

For me, living abroad at such a formative time in my life, at ages 19 and 22, I believe I somewhat grew up in these countries and learned how to fend for myself. While it was a relatively short period of time, it was impactful. In the Dominican Republic, not having my parents to lean on, I learned how to manage my money, date, and be a responsible college student and adult, who handled my responsibilities, didn't get into trouble or worse—get hurt or do things to put my life in danger. I made a few bad decisions there that I learned from.

Living in Colombia, for the first time flaunting my natural curly hair in an afro in public, I learned how to love myself, and my God-given beauty. I became fearless. I didn't care about the stares. It was a thrilling experience, and to this day, I feel like my afro protected me. That was my first job as a college graduate. I had bills to pay, such as rent, water and electricity. It was there where I learned how to be a responsible adult who could work hard, make an impact on students, but also travel and enjoy life. My experience abroad also helped me to understand more of what it meant to be an American and the privileges that come with it.

We, as Americans, often take for granted the fact that we can travel to almost anywhere in the world without a visa. We have immense freedoms, from access to free education, to a free press, to our right to protest. Even if someone is living in public housing, they still live in a finished building with running water and floors better than concrete. Many of them receive assistance with buying food. Simple things, such as hot water and electricity, we as Americans tend to take for granted. Food stamps even.

In other countries, if you don't have any money, you starve, or you eat things like plantains and rice every day. Also, affirmative action, and the help that is out there for students of color is not as standard abroad. While African Americans still have quite the fight toward equality in the United States, living abroad made me realize we are doing a hell of a lot better than some of our brothers and sisters who were brought over as slaves to other countries on the American continents. These experiences gave me a new perspective on life.

I wouldn't be where I am today without these experiences. I not only studied Spanish in college, I lived over there. My stays abroad allowed me to experience and witness the culture firsthand. And these experiences have helped me obtain every job I've had in the United States since I've returned.

When I meet people from these areas, we share common experiences and form an instant bond. The memories created there will last forever. It is so thrilling to be dropped off in a foreign place and find your way.

Living back in the United States, especially as a journalist, the experiences I've had are unparalleled. When I cover stories on immigration, I have a deeper understanding of the issues they face. I've stayed overnight in homes with concrete floors, flimsy roofs, cockroaches and no running water. I've stayed for days in places where electricity was a bonus. I've met with people displaced by war and had conversations with them.

Going abroad will give you so much more understanding of humanity. While you can't help but compare the differences between cultures, you are sure to be amazed by how much we have in common and develop a much deeper understanding for humanity—along with the ability to love people for not where they come from, but for who they are inside.

Glossary

Amigo (a) – friend
Blanquear la raza – whiten the race
Bogotános – people from Bogotá, Colombia
Botellas de agua – bottled wáter
Cajero – ATM
Cédula – identification card
Chiva – party bus
Conchos – public car
Corbata – tie
Gordita – chubby girl
Grave – serious
Guagua – van
Jefe (a) – boss, leader
Los Estados Unidos – the United States
Moto – scooter
Perejil – parsley
Plátanos – plantains
Puesto de chequeo – checkpoint
Se fue la luz – out went the lights, electricity
Si Dios quiere – God-willing

Stephanie Claytor

Acknowledgments

Of course this incredible journey would not be possible without the people who supported me along the way. I want to thank my parents for not smothering me and allowing me to explore the world on my own terms. My mother made it a priority for our family to take a vacation to a new state every summer, thus sparking my love for traveling.

I want to thank my friend, Dariana, for taking me on my first trip outside the mainland to Puerto Rico and further instilling my joy for traveling and learning Spanish. She taught me all of the Latin dances, which really helped me learn more about the culture.

I want to thank my Dominican host mom and sister for taking such good care of me. My host sister was the first person to tell me about the program that allowed me to teach abroad in Colombia. She also vouched for my Spanish, helping me to get selected.

I want to thank my American friends in the Dominican Republic and Colombia for watching over me and making sure I didn't get into too much trouble.

I thank my editor for pushing me to finish this book and I thank God for giving me the courage and vision to tell my story.

I thank my husband for giving me the time and tools to finish the book.

Lastly, I want to thank my Spanish teachers at Twinsburg High School and at Syracuse University for helping me to learn a second language that has opened so many doors.

To my second-grade teacher, Carol Zenisek, this book is for you. She traveled to every continent and shared pictures with her students. I was hooked from then on. My only regret is I failed to respond to her letter and meet with her upon my return from Colombia. She passed away a few years later.

Stephanie Claytor

About the Author

Known for keeping journals as a child and telling funny stories, Stephanie Claytor has spent much of her life writing in her spare time and professionally. The Central Florida resident was born and raised in Twinsburg, Ohio, a suburb of Cleveland. She went on to graduate from Syracuse University's S.I. Newhouse School of Public Communications summa cum laude, with honors. While attending college, she majored in Broadcast Journalism, International Relations with a geographic concentration on Latin America, and Spanish Language, Literature, and Culture. After studying abroad in the Dominican Republic during college, she earned a Fulbright English Teaching Assistantship and was stationed in Bogota, Colombia.

When she returned home, Stephanie went on to pursue her dream job of becoming a television reporter and multimedia journalist, covering stories in states across the South and Midwest, including in New Mexico, Louisiana, Texas, Missouri, Iowa, and Florida. Her talents as a videographer, writer and video editor led to her becoming a Florida Associated Press Broadcasters award-winning Multi-Media Reporter. While she thrived in her broadcasting career, Stephanie still felt a desire to sit down and write her first book about her time living abroad and everything she experienced that shaped much of the rest of her life.

In the process of writing and editing this book, she created the travel and lifestyle blog, www.blacktrekking.com. Through the blog, she details her travels around the world, and offers travelers tips to make their trips more enjoyable. So far, she's visited numerous countries, including Japan, Ghana, and France, and three territories including Bora Bora, Puerto Rico, and Turks and Caicos.

Connect Online:

www.blacktrekking.com

Facebook.com/blacktrekking
Twitter.com/blacktrekking
Instagram.com/blacktrekking

blacktrekking@gmail.com

Stephanie Claytor

CPSIA information can be obtained
at www.ICGtesting.com
Printed in the USA
FSHW021235130719
59960FS